MW01025636

To Steve & Cathy,
May my journey bless &
inspire you!

Kate

Paralyzed
but not
Powerless

Kate's Journey Revisited

Birthday Wisher Steve,
a special Month!

Kate Adamson

I'm lucky to have a mum like you.
I'm glad you're still here.
I like the way you are.

– Rachel

What happens when you have to suddenly be responsible?
Mum had a stroke when I was just three years old.
Mum, I'm so glad you survived.

– Stephanie

Paralyzed
but not
Powerless

Kate's Journey revisited

Kate Adamson
With her husband's observations
"From the Other Side of the Bed"

Nosmada Press
Redondo Beach, California

Dedicated to stroke survivors,
their families, friends and advocates.

Paralyzed but not Powerless
Kate's Journey revisited
With her husband's observations "From the Other Side of the Bed"
Copyright © 2008 by Kate Adamson, Second Edition

ISBN: 978-0-9741907-0-9
$19.95 U.S.

Publisher's Cataloging in Publication Data available upon request.
Printed and bound in the United States of America

Cover Design: Dotti Albertine
Cover Photo: Dani Brubaker
Text Design: Sheryl Mehary

Nosmada Press
409 North Pacific Coast Highway
PMB 415
Redondo Beach, California 90277

Contents

Prologue

I Am Dead

*I*t's not shiny or bright.

No past life goes rushing by.

No one waits for me at the end of a tunnel.

This is not like near death experiences I've heard about. Other peoples' hearts stopped, sending them down a path toward the light.

My heart is fine, beating away; its beat is killing my brain. My brain has begun to decerebrate. My microprocessor is being fried, the wiring burning up at the speed of light. The pain is unbelievable. Everything is falling away from me like autumn leaves in the wind. Now, I cannot move my arms or legs. Now, I cannot talk. Now, I cannot even blink my eyes!

I see and hear everything going on around me but there is no link whatsoever with my body. I am alive – in here – somewhere – but where? I cannot make even the simplest movements, locked in a rigid fetal position. Look at me. I am a 33-year-old fetus, going out just as I came in.

I don't know what is happening, except I am dying. My children are terrified. So am I. Thoughts of my little ones fill my dying brain. I can hear Stephanie fighting and screaming, "Give me back my mommy, you can't take her. I want Mom!"

The paramedics can't respond to her; they are busy doing their job. Death stands silently nearby. No matter how Stephanie screams for her mom, Death is not obliged to answer. Death is no stranger to the men with my life in their hands. They pay no attention to Death standing in the shadows. The paramedics can do little, but they will try everything – and there is no time for bedside manners.

No one cares if I am scared. They don't have time. They only care if I live. "We are losing her!"

Now there is no time to reach UCLA, the best place for a stroke victim. Faltering vital signs allow no choice, the radio crackles. A static-beleaguered voice diverts the ambulance to the nearest hospital. It is a good hospital, but small. The chance for cutting edge treatment is gone. No MRI. No chance anyone will figure out in time what is happening to me. My best chance is gone.

The paramedics are undecided. Should they go to sirens or just allow me to finish dying quietly? My youth and excellent physical condition makes it inappropriate to just let me "go peacefully into that good night." Sirens wail as they hit the accelerator. Good. I will "rage (and rage some more) against the dying of the light." I do not welcome Death. I didn't invite him. I will not even acknowledge him. But Death has my attention.

Jangled and confused information comes in from the outside. Everything is foggy and blurred except for the unbearable pain which is crystal clear, a knife with a glittering steel blade floating in cold, black, starless space.

My heart pumps fast and strong; each pump sending a deadly trickle of blood through a leaking artery to kill more and more brain cells.

The cells in my midbrain that route all electrical impulses to and from my brain are drowned in blood. Here in the pons area, there are no two sides to this part of the brain; there is no backup system. I should be terrified, but even fear can't enter this place through my shorted-out switchboard.

I live my life by a day planner. I see the schedule for next week in bold red ink, or is that blood? 11 a.m. – funeral. 1 p.m. – 2 p.m. eternity. NO! I want to live. But what if I do survive? Will I throw my planner off schedule? I'm moving fast now. Where am I going?

I understand nothing. My head is effectively severed from my body. Brainstem to main brain: "We are closing down. Let's go home."

But I am too young to die; so here we go – sirens, lights and speed. I am moving somewhere very fast. Where am I going?

Oh, I see a sign ahead. It reads "Eternity."

I am in a coffin made of glass. I see and hear everything. I am shut off from everyone and everything. Hours and days go by. My only companions are the constant thoughts running through my mind.

Who is here in this place? Is it me? Do I exist? Is God here with me? Where am I? Is this eternity?

There is no time in this place, but there is pain. Thus, pain becomes the reality and eternity becomes the clock. The clock that never ends – silently not ticking.

I am so desperately alone. I want this to end. Maybe it already has. God, are you there? I hear no response – nothing. No answer, no feeling – just a lot of nothing. This is not real. I begin to doubt my own existence. Maybe this is what it is like not to exist. Maybe even God doesn't talk to people who don't exist.

But I feel pain – therefore, I must be real. Where are you God? How could you let this happen? Show yourself! Please! I will keep your mystery to myself. I will not tell your secret, for I can tell no one anything. Please help me. I need to see you, touch you. At least talk to me. Say something, do something, heal me, help me!

More days have gone by. Where am I? Where have I gone? Eternity? But Eternity is undecided whether it wants me. Eternity can bring relief from pain, maybe even bringing peace. Eternity cannot end. Eternity will last forever.

All I can do is think. I think and think – then I think and think some more. It is all I can do – "I think therefore I am." Where have I heard that? Hey, wait! I can think – therefore I am! I exist. I must exist.

Well, okay then; I am real. Then it is back to talking to God. I never prayed much before, but now, I have all the time in the world to pray. Praying is the only thing I can do. I can think, but I can't talk – except to God. I'll think and think and talk and talk, to God. Maybe God will get tired of it and I will get some action.

Maybe God will drop me a rope so I can climb out of this pit, but how would that help anyway? I have no use of my hands, so I can't hold onto the rope.

If I can't grab onto a rope, then maybe, God could lasso me and pull me out. That would be fine with me. I want so much for this to end, but wait; then I would have to leave my babies. No deal. I would do anything to have that miracle, anything but leave my children. So I keep on going. I'm not going to quit.

Wait, I just felt something. There it is again – a tiny spark – maybe just a bit brighter now. What is it? It is hope. As long as there is a spark of hope for this paralyzed body, I will fan it with my un-paralyzed mind.

Visitors come and visitors go. "This is only for a season," friends tell me. Then they ask each other if I can even hear them. A season? Winter is a season. When you look at it through double-pane glass, sipping hot cocoa before a fire at a ski lodge, winter is a season. It is eternity when you are lost in the dark, in a blizzard without a coat.

Why am I going through this? Is there a purpose to it? What is God's plan? I wish He would let me in on it. Any plan is better than the one I haven't got.

Life goes on around me. Days pass, weeks, and still no signal in and no signal out. I am dead. There is not a doubt about that. I am entombed in my own body – sealed in a glass coffin. I want to scream, "I am still me!"

I remember stories of spring time, another empty tomb and, who can say, maybe I too will live again. It is very possible because I have hope. Yes, it is very possible that from my death, I too will be reborn. "Kate, come forth!" What a day that will be. What or whom will I be when I come forth?

More time passes. No signal in and no signal out. They still think I am dead. But the joke is on them because I discovered I can think. Now, I know I exist. Thank you Descartes! I can talk to God, and if God listens, I may live again. It's possible, it must be. I have hope – doesn't that make it possible? Okay God, here's the deal, let me live! I may never be the same, but I am willing to be different. I was once Kate Adamson, Katie, Mum or Mrs. Klugman. You may not let me be any of those people again, but I am someone. Please God, let me be someone.

Rachel, 18 months
Stephanie, 3 years

Foreword

$\mathcal{T}$ he *pons* is the neuroanatomical term for bridge. It is that part of the brainstem that connects the brain with all the electrical traffic coming in, that allows us to feel, and all the traffic out, that allows us to speak and move.

When Kate was thirty-three years old, in the full bloom of health and youth, she suffered a *pontine stroke,* and this bridge was short-circuited in blood totally paralyzing her from head to toe. Suddenly, this independent, lively spirit became trapped in her paralyzed body. She was helpless and alone as her formerly healthy, beautifully fit body, withered to skin and bones.

This is the story of Kate's excruciatingly slow and courageous journey from despair to hope and recovery. With unbelievable strength and determination; first to survive, then to let go, change, adapt, and finally to thrive.

Kate remembers all the voices of belief, encouragement and faith that helped her build her own bridge to recovery. Voices of her God, voices of friends and family, caring professionals, and her own voice.

Kate's left arm remains paralyzed, walking is still a major effort, and stroke-resultant depression is a frequent visitor, but she reaches out to others. She founded a support group for stroke survivors like herself and speaks out on behalf of stroke survivors in national forums. She is a nationally recognized public speaker, presenting her unique outlook on how to overcome the paralysis that keeps individuals and organizations from moving to their next level of purpose and accomplishment. She emphasizes the importance of appreciation before accommodation in meeting legally required accommodation requirements – recognizing and appreciating the valuable traits in those who successfully deal with disabling circumstances and appreciating valuable contributions they can make. In her book, Kate offers information, insights, encouragement and hope.

I first met Kate in Los Angeles, California at Rancho Los Amigos National Rehabilitation Center in 1996. On several occasions I had been a guest speaker at the "Back on Track" support group that she founded in Redondo Beach, California.

It has truly been an honor and inspiration to know Kate and to share a small part of her life's work.

Helena Chui, M.D. – Chair of the Department of Neurology,
University of Southern California, Keck School of Medicine.

Chapter One

~

On the Wings of Youth

I was raised on a large sheep ranch in the South Island of New Zealand. Dad was a shepherd and Mum cooked for the farm hands. They had four of us under the age of five: my two older brothers, Tony and Rodney, and my twin sister, Lynn, and me.

Mum learned she was having twins just six weeks before we were born. Her doctor told her he could hear two hearts beating. When she told Dad the news, he almost collapsed. "How are we going to manage four little ones under five?"

"It will be fine," Mum replied, "we'll manage" – and manage they did.

When I was two years old, my parents moved to Dunedin, a beautiful city of red tile roofs and large backyard vegetable gardens. Quaint city homes are surrounded by lush green hills. Dunedin is one of the largest cities in New Zealand. The people are wonderful, 180,000 friendly, helpful neighbors. There, my parents built the home they still live in today.

Dad returned to his original trade as a furniture polisher and opened a business called Hi-Glo Polishing. It was hard for my parents to manage the care of young children on their limited income, so, Mum worked three days a week in a yarn shop to make ends meet.

My parents grew much of our food in the backyard garden and Mum made her own jam and preserves to save money. She was a wonderful cook. One of my favorite memories is coming home for dinner to the aroma of garden fresh vegetables.

Wednesday was baking day. She filled the cake tins with tasty goodies. After school, we would often bring friends home who loved Mum's baking. They wished their mothers could bake like her! I have happy recollections of seeing her, sitting at the kitchen window, stirring a huge pot of jam that filled the house with mouth-watering aroma.

They did the best they could for us, and it seemed pretty good to me. My parents wanted a better life for us – and the earlier we could get started the better. When I was six years old, Mum enrolled us all in speech lessons with Miss Lawrence. She was a heavy-set, no-nonsense woman with strawberry colored hair pulled up and held in place with hairpins. She was personally disheveled, but exacting about her passion – clear, precise, and proper speech. "Elocution," she called it.

Miss Lawrence had a small private studio in the heart of town in an area known as the Octagon. It is surrounded by green, broadleaf trees. From the window of the studio you could see a statue of the famous poet, Robert Burns.

The lessons were more than just speaking, drama, or acting, they were about communicating. At the advice of Miss Lawrence, we entered speech and drama competitions. Our school holidays were taken up with preparations. Countless nights Mum would sit by the heater outlet in the hallway of our home listening to our lines as one by one we went into the hall to rehearse.

I remember performing "Topsy" from Uncle Tom's Cabin. When it was time for competition Mum rubbed theatrical black stick on my face and hands and tied my hair up in rags torn in long strips from an old bed sheet. In those days, we didn't know the meaning of politically correct. In my young eyes, everyone was a character and the dramatic context of every life was interesting.

I loved being on stage and really being the character I was portraying. I often wonder if it was my stage training that helped me step outside my own feelings, and put on the happy mask for the world, whenever things turned upside down in my life.

My twin sister, Lynn, invariably got stage fright when it was her turn to go on and she would just clam up. So Mum pushed me on stage without giving me a moment to think about it. Suddenly, I was staring at what must have been a thousand faces staring right back at me. I could barely see them through the stage lights shining brightly in my eyes – but they were out there!

I had butterflies in my stomach for the first few minutes. Then, I remembered my speech teacher's words, "Take a deep breath, relax, and deliver your lines one word at a time." I opened my mouth and the words came out like a brave little army; a steady flow marching in order like disciplined soldiers, I was the general and I was in command! My teacher's coaching combined with my mother's faith in me worked, and at six years old, I felt wonderfully brilliant and charismatic.

I seemed to have a gift for language and drama. I loved the stage and was happy to let my life revolve around school and speech classes. Then my teenage years hit. And yes, I was a typical teenager – resistant to other's instructions, yet unsure of myself. I was confused about what I wanted out of life. At 19, restless and uncomfortable in my own skin, having fun with my friends was more important to me than academic achievement.

At a New Year's Eve party in 1980, I met an American boy, and fell in love as only a 19-year-old can. Surely, I had found true love – he was the one! He asked me to go to the United States with him. Here was a chance to ride off into the sunset and live happily ever after with my Prince Charming (hmm-m-m-m, well, America was east of New Zealand, so I guess I should say ride off into the sunrise). My parents were dead set against my leaving New Zealand, but I was determined to go. I had never been out of the country. At 19, all distances seemed short and all obstacles easily surmountable. I was young and headstrong. I knew what was best for me. The best thing for me was to see the world with my one true love.

Of course, life doesn't always work out the way we plan or demand. I left my old problems behind only to gain a whole new set of problems. Running away doesn't really change anything, except your address. Every time we change partners, jobs, homes, cities or countries, we just change one set of problems for another, and they don't get solved until we turn and face them. I didn't know that then, and just moving on seemed to be the right thing to do.

As someone later said, "On the wings of youth, Kate flew into the unknown." My journey took me from New Zealand to California and then to London. Two years later, when things didn't work out as I had planned, I flew from London back to California. The man I thought was Mr. Right turned out to be more like Mr. Ed (of course it was all his fault – after all, I was perfect). That was okay, because I, as usual, had an escape plan. My "plan B" was to be an au pair (nanny) in London.

I was excited about the London family I would be living with. The nanny agency in New Zealand said I would have my own room with a TV and the use of a car. It all sounded perfect. I imagined Robert Young and Donna Reed as my new employers, and that I would be taking care of the adorable, witty, talented children from *Mary Poppins.*

I arrived at Heathrow Airport in London to find my new family waiting for me, holding a large sign reading "Adamson." We picked up my luggage and drove on the autobahn to their suburb. Susan, the mother, helped settle me into my new room. "Would you like some supper?" she asked.

"Oh, no thanks, I'm not hungry," I said politely. I soon learned that "supper" in England means "dinner" (in New Zealand we called it "tea"). I was in a different country now with a different language, so I went to bed hungry, without supper, dinner, tea or anything. I realized that I had better learn the cultural slang quickly, or I would starve.

The nanny job lasted three months. It wasn't quite what I thought it was going to be. The children were brats and the house was situated in the path of airplane traffic. Every three minutes jet airplanes flew overhead, causing the dishes and silverware to dance like the cutlery and the teapot in *Beauty and the Beast.*

Susan always had a long "to do" list to keep me busy and out of trouble. I could use the car only to take the children to school and home. My luxurious bedroom was a small room with a tiny black and white TV with a loose antenna. At mealtime, I had to eat with the children. I had to prepare the family meals and clean up after everyone. At 19, I was a wife and mother, with none of the perks. This was harder on them, because I didn't know a thing about cooking.

When the London family planned their summer vacation to Greece, I was excited about going along as the nanny. My hopes were dashed when Susan told me that I was to stay home and take care of things, and I, of course, wouldn't be getting paid for that week either.

I did get on well with the husband. He had a wonderful sense of humor, and as long as I would sit and listen to his jokes and stories, I didn't have to work. Then one night Susan came to my room and told me to be seen and not heard. Apparently, Robert Young was looking for Lolita, and Donna Reed was jealous. But whatever their issues and suspicions, this was the final straw for me. *Me! Kate? Seen and not heard? Yeah, right!* I don't know how I lasted even three months.

I had another nanny friend from Australia. Jean was having problems with her family as well. We decided to skip out, and go to London looking for work. "Where will we live Jean?" I asked concerned.

"Let's get out of here. We'll take it one step at a time," she said optimistically.

While my host family slept, I quietly packed my things.

The next morning, I went about my usual morning duties, my heart racing in anticipation and nervousness. I took the kids to school then waited nervously for the parents to leave. Susan handed me a list. As she did, she paused and gave me a piercing look for a long minute, as if she knew something was up. Then she seemed to shrug off whatever she was thinking, handed me the list and went bustling about in preparation for leaving for the airport. Her mother-in-law was coming to stay and she wanted things in order.

Mid-morning, I heard the honk of a taxicab. I grabbed my suitcase, ran outside and jumped into the cab. I felt like a runaway slave on the Underground Railroad.

Wow, I did it! I can't believe I'm doing this! I breathed a sigh of relief as the cab pulled out of the driveway. *Free, free, free at last!* Just then, Susan drove up in her car with her mother-in-law. When she saw the cab driving off, she jumped out of her car and started running after the cab screaming, "You can't do this to me! I need help! You can't do this!"

"Go, go, go, GO!" I screamed at the cab driver who floored the old cab and roared out of the driveway. Dust and gravel spurted from underneath the rear tires like the tails of twin comets.

I met Jean downtown at a posh fish-and-chips restaurant called Flanagan's. We couldn't afford lunch but we did need jobs so we asked for the manager. The manager had us fill out applications and asked about our experience in the restaurant business. The most experience I had at that point in my life was carrying dirty dishes from the kitchen table to the kitchen counter. *How hard could this be?* We were cute and convincing, the manager hired us both.

I took to the job like a duck takes to water. I loved interacting with people and my acting classes served me well. I spent two years in London working at the restaurant and traveling as often as I could. Jean and I found a suburb that housed Australians and New Zealanders so we could preserve our heritage – our accent!

I also worked at El Vino's wine bar; I have never had so much fun. My co-workers and I still stay in touch. Their memories of me are of the good-time girl – always ready to party, shop and have a laugh. I was having the time of my life; however, as much as I liked London, I did not see myself putting down roots there. My passport was running out and I decided to return to New Zealand.

On my way back to New Zealand, I visited some friends in Los Angeles, whom I had met during my first visit there two years earlier. For six weeks, I basked in the Palm Springs sun. Life just could not get any better. I decided to stay in Los Angeles. My ticket home had been canceled with no refund, so I only had $300 in my pocket. When did I ever worry about tomorrow? I had seen plenty of movies about the small town girl making good in the big city. And I was just as cute and smart as any of them.

As I struggled to support myself as a waitress, I met Duncan, a Midwest guy from Kansas City, now in the real estate business in California. I was a little more cautious this time. We dated for a couple of years before getting married in Las Vegas. I continued my waitress job, but I wanted more.

Another waitress at the Velvet Turtle was a Mary Kay consultant. She talked about sales meetings and the prizes she was winning while making money at the same time. *I can do this.* I went to one of the sales meetings and signed up as a Mary Kay beauty consultant.

"Wow," I thought, "I am a consultant!"

As naïve as that sounds, I went at this new venture with the zeal of youth. I had business cards made and took them everywhere I went. I handed out five cards a day like I was told to do. It worked. It really did. I began to make money right away.

I went everywhere with my pink bags and my free car. Driving the California freeways was a real challenge for this Kiwi girl. I was used to driving on the other side of the road. I enjoyed my new career. I became a director. We called our team, "The Down Under Wonders."

The marriage with Duncan lasted only four years (we are still good friends today). It was hard to stay focused and keep my business going while dealing with the divorce. I had to sell a lot of product just to keep the car. It was too much for me.

I went back to working in the restaurant business. My Mary Kay career had taught me a lot, especially discipline and an attitude of persistence that still serves me well in my speaking business. It may well have helped me through the dark valley of paralysis, through which I would one day be forced to walk. I have many friends who have remained in the profession.

I met my second husband, Steven, in 1990. He was a personal injury attorney practicing in Century City. Steven was (and is) brilliant and witty, with a wonderful mind. He is a lot of fun. We became great friends. I found myself spending more and more time with him, going places and doing things, whatever crossed our minds. In 1991 we got married. Thirteen days later I threw up.

Yep, I was pregnant with our first child.

~

Many readers have expressed how much they appreciated the inserts from Dr. Jeffrey Saver, which helped them understand, from a medical view, what was happening to me and those who have had similar experiences.

Others have asked me what was happening with my family. So, I asked my husband Steven to share with you directly and personally what was happening from the other side of the hospital bed. He agreed to tell you how he felt as he experienced his own journey by my side.

Always remember, that the terror and trauma of stroke – or any devastating illness or injury – affects more than just the patient. Family takes the first and hardest hit, then friends and business associates. In this edition, I thought it would be appropriate for my husband to weigh in, once in a while, with his observations and feelings about dealing with my trauma and the new person who came home to him.

I appreciate Steven doing this for me, as I think you will appreciate his comments.

From the Other Side of the Bed

*S*omeone, I can't remember who, once said "I was born at a very early age." I was born in Minnesota. World War II had ended two years earlier on my birthday August 14. I got out of the frigid North when I was six, when my family moved to California.

I was a precocious child – much too smart for my own good. This is not my story so I don't want to go into great detail about my own life. I do want to tell you about something that prepared me to understand and deal with what would one day happen to my beautiful wife – and would make me a believer in her and fight for her in ways that seem to go beyond reason.

One winter day I got sick. First, it was just a little fever, then it was a lot of fever and then, suddenly I was paralyzed. Like so many other kids during the great polio epidemic, I had gone swimming in the wrong lake, at the wrong time.

The point is, that I recovered. I wasn't supposed to. The odds were against me. My doctor didn't think I would, but I did. I did much more and much better than was expected. I remembered how difficult it was; working hours and hours just to regain the coordination to bounce a ball.

I am not trying to get your sympathy by telling you how tough it was for me. Most kids have to overcome something, and a lot of kids have to get through some pretty tough stuff. My experience was, I think, designed especially for me so I would believe in miracles – and give doctors respect, but not reverence.

It was a critical attitude that helped me, as Kate's advocate, deal with a sometimes insensitive and unbelieving medical profession. Throughout Kate's Journey through hell, I believed in her and fought for her right to *live. After all, if they were wrong about me in 1954 why couldn't they be wrong about her in 1995.*

Chapter Two

~

Glass Coffin

Giving birth to my first child, Stephanie, was a wonderful and horrendous experience. The labor? Horrendous! The results? Wonderful! After four days of labor with no outcome, I was finally given an emergency Cesarean section – and gave birth to a healthy, kickin' eight pound bundle of raw energy. Stephanie was excited to join the family and I was ecstatic to join the ranks of motherhood.

I was back in the gym six weeks after giving birth. I had always been a health fanatic, staying physically fit was a top priority. As soon as my gynecologist gave me the clearance, I returned to working out. He placed me on a very low-dosage birth control pill that had minimal side effects.

After the birth of Stephanie, I started suffering migraine headaches and also started losing weight. I began experiencing nervousness and my hair started falling out. An endocrinologist ran some tests, including a blood panel and an ultrasound on my thyroid, which had completely shut down. I had developed a rare condition called Thyroiditis. I was about to begin a regimen of medication when my thyroid suddenly started up again as if nothing had happened. I set the experience aside as just one of the medical mysteries of life and didn't think much more about it.

In December of 1993, our second daughter, Rachel, was ready to come into the world. Because of the Thyroiditis and previous complications, my doctor scheduled another Cesarean. I knew ahead of time what was in store for me and was prepared for the ordeal. By this time in my life, I had developed the attitude that physical strength, and vitality, was the answer to all life's trials. And I was fit to be tried!

Nine days before Christmas, Rachel Elizabeth Klugman joined our family. This tiny beautiful baby weighed no more than six pounds. She had the most delicate features and was like an exquisite porcelain doll. What a wonderful Christmas gift!

Like a professional athlete, well conditioned, I was ready for it and I bounced back quickly. The same symptoms I had experienced after Stephanie's birth also bounced back. I waited it out and, sure enough, full function of that tricky little gland returned three months after Rachel's birth.

Again, I didn't think much of it. I would just keep in shape. That would solve everything, right? I waited impatiently for clearance from my doctor, then went back on birth control and back to the gym. Weeks turned into months and life continued on as usual.

Life was perfect. I had a new baby. I lived in a five bedroom home, exclusive California neighborhood, with my successful attorney husband and my two adorable daughters. Everything was perfect. Well, except for those headaches.

When Rachel was 17 months old, my headaches started again. They felt like migraines. I was sure that was all it was. I had had them before. This time I assumed it was a result of the flare-up of my thyroid condition. I had massages, took long relaxing baths and continued working out. I would take over-the-counter medication and lie down in a dark, quiet room with a cold compress on my head until the pain subsided. I saw the wonderful month of June through a heavy gloss of pain. I found it hard to participate in the normal events of life, but somehow I continued my daily activities trying to ignore the pain and focus on being a wife and mother.

Keeping a house in order was like threading beads on a string with no knot at the end. I was continuously trying to keep up with my to-do list in spite of how I felt. *I'll feel better soon.* I relied on my friends to help me with the girls so I could rest and relieve the pain.

In mid-June, I finally responded to my husband's constant requests to get medical attention. Steven wanted me to see my regular doctor but I felt he was too far away to drive. I made the fateful decision to seek help from a chiropractor instead of a trained medical doctor.

That choice will haunt me for the rest of my life.

The chiropractor assured me that adjustments to my neck would help get rid of the headaches. They didn't. My headaches became worse. The chiropractor did not diagnose that I was having a stroke.

Some days the pain was unbearable. My head felt like it was going to explode. I cried – a lot. In the mornings, I would feel some slight relief. Maybe it was because I was a morning person and was talking myself into feeling better. I continued with my daily activities trying to block out the pain, focusing on being a good wife and mother, and continue my daily routine of exercise. *It will get better, I just need to be patient.*

On the morning of June 29, I woke up with that nasty headache. I just wanted to stay in bed, but I had promised a girlfriend that I would work out with her. So, despite how I felt, I decided to meet her. After all, I couldn't let her down. *I'll just try my best to work through this. At least the endorphins might help and I can get my mind off the pain.*

The children played in the kids club while we worked out. My headache got worse. I decided not to push a strenuous workout and just did a little walking on the treadmill before picking up my daughters and going home.

That afternoon, Stephanie had a birthday party to attend. I decided to just drop her off and go home to lie down. *A nap will help me feel better.*

Before picking Stephanie up, I stopped for coffee. I ran into a couple of gym-buddies who asked if I was feeling okay. They said I was looking pretty stressed. I laughed it off, thanking them for the "compliment," then left to get my daughter.

On Wednesday evenings, I normally went with Steven to my regular small church group, but this time I didn't feel well enough to attend. My headache was getting worse and worse. "Go ahead without me, I'm going to bed early to shake this headache," I told him. Steven took both girls with him, leaving me to relax.

Cherri and I planned to meet the next morning at the mall for a puppet show with the kids. That night I called her in tears.

"Cherri, this is the worst headache I have ever had," I said, my voice shaking. "I need to take a hot bath and go to bed. I'll see you tomorrow, okay?"

"Kate, quit trying to be tough. You have been having these headaches for way too long. You really need to call a doctor."

She was right. Steven had begged me to get medical attention. They were both right. I hung up the phone. *She's right. This has gone on too long. I will call my doctor in the morning.*

From the Other Side of the Bed

*K*ate *is so stubborn. I tried and tried to get her to go to the doctor. I thought the problem was that she was working out too much and was too thin. What else could be wrong at 33? How could a woman with a perfect diet who worked out three or four times a week, two or three hours at time, be sick? That she could be having something as serious as a stroke never even crossed my mind.*

I threatened to stay home and not to go to work if she did not go to the doctor, but she called my bluff. She had (has) an amazing tolerance for pain. She grew up with this Spartan attitude that you never went to the doctor unless you had already died.

I finally got so concerned that I pulled out the prescription information from Kate's birth control pills and there it was, "Migraine headaches." I called her gynecologist and pleaded with him to see her immediately. He refused, telling us to wait until after the Fourth of July holiday. But this year, for Kate, my children and me there would be no celebration of fireworks.

While soaking in the tub, the pain started climbing off the charts. It felt like my head was going to explode. I covered my face and cried into the washcloth. Before climbing into bed, I took a mild sleeping pill. *I sure hope I feel better in the morning.* I drifted off into a deep sleep.

The alarm startled me awake at six. I got out of bed, walked into my bathroom and started running the water for a shower. I still had a dull, lingering headache; but there was no time to worry about that now. I had a lot of work ahead of me and had to get things ready. With Rachel still in diapers, I needed to prepare a diaper bag and snacks.

As I was showering, waves of dizziness swept over me. *I'll probably feel better after I eat something.*

I stepped out of the shower, and started to put on my pajamas so I could stay warm while I dried my hair. As I stepped into my pajama bottoms, my left leg started to give way under me. I felt weird and weak, like my muscles had turned to jelly.

I had no strength to stand up. An odd feeling swept through my body, sucking the strength out of me. The sensation startled me. I reached out to steady myself against the counter. *That's odd. I think I better sit down for a minute.* I sat on the marble ledge surrounding my bathtub. *This doesn't seem right. I'd better lie down. I must be coming down with something.*

Struggling into my pajama top, I staggered to my bed and flopped down like a rag doll. I turned my head and looked over at my husband sleeping soundly. *This feels like a bad dream.* I tried to conceal my fear. "Wake up, Steven, wake up. I feel really bad." He just mumbled sleepily and rolled over on his side. "Steven, please, something is wrong. I don't feel well," I told him.

In a groggy voice he said, "Let me sleep, I'll drive you to see the doctor later," he said, pulling the covers over his head.

"No! Please wake up. I need help now," I said, panicking. "Something's really wrong!"

Steven immediately sat up, "What is it? Is it one of the kids?"

"I need help," I exclaimed.

Those were the last words I spoke out loud for many months.

He grabbed the phone and dialed the neighbors. "Rocky! Something's wrong with Kate! I need to take her to the doctor right now. Can you and Doreen come over and sit with the kids?"

Steven tried not to show his shock and disbelief. He turned to me and spoke reassuringly, "Okay Kate, Rocky and Doreen are on their way over." *On their way over! I need to button my pajama top. What's happening? My left arm won't move!*

Frustrated and frightened, I tried to scream out. *What's happening? Why can't you understand me? I need help now! What's Rocky going to do?*

I was speaking clearly in my head, but only a stream of slurred sounds came out. *I don't want to be sick! Please God don't let there be anything wrong!* Something was already wrong – very wrong. Paralysis was sweeping through my body like a tide of death.

The doorbell rang and Steven hurried to let our neighbors in. Rocky took one look at me and said, "Dial 911 immediately." Now I was terrified. *Dear God, what is happening to me. Help.*

I heard the sound of sirens and heavy footsteps on the stairs. "In here," shouted Steven. The paramedics quickly assembled a stretcher and cautiously eased me onto it. Rocky, Doreen and my husband stood back, concern written all over their faces.

The ambulance attendants carefully maneuvered the stretcher downstairs. *Hey, be careful of the walls. What are you doing? Why are you making such a big deal about this? This is embarrassing. Such fuss! I can walk down these stairs.*

Little did I know that I would never walk normally again. My legs were already completely paralyzed.

Neighbors gathered outside their houses to watch. *What is going to happen to me?*

The paramedic reached for an oxygen mask. "Relax, Mrs. Klugman, I just need to give you some oxygen. Try to take deep breaths." I followed his instructions. Whatever it was, I knew deep inside, that my life had taken a hard turn – and it wasn't good.

Stephanie and Rachel were at the bottom of the stairs. Doreen was holding Stephanie's hand and Rachel was in her arms, crying. "What's wrong with Mommy?" Stephanie asked.

I'll never forget the look on her face or the sight of my little girls in the early morning darkness as I was taken away in the ambulance. *I'll be home soon. My babies! My babies!*

The words to an old song began playing in my head. "*Hello darkness my old friend. I've come to talk to you again …*"

In the emergency room, I was disoriented, bewildered, confused, and frightened beyond belief. I could hear people talking, but I couldn't respond. *Please somebody help! I'm scared. What's happening to me? Why can't I say what I am thinking?*

The ER doctor didn't think I could be having a stroke. "She's too young and healthy," he told my husband. None of the doctors knew what was happening.

In an act of caution, the doctor hooked me up to a respirator. This meant I had to be intubated. Tubes had to go down my nose to my lungs – a horrible, painful procedure. They lowered my blood pressure, slowing down my bleeding. I was in a world where a tenth of a second and a millimeter of space made the difference between life and death. With my normal blood pressure, I would have died in minutes.

Groping for a cause, the doctor, attempted a CT (Computerized Tomography) scan of my brain. Although making conventional sense, he was looking for the cause in entirely the wrong place. That's like looking for Yellowstone National Park in New York!

The CT scan results appeared to be normal, so the doctor took me off the respirator pulled the tube out of my lungs, through my nose and attempted to waken me. I could hear this voice and feel him gently nudging me. "Kate, wake up if you can hear me. Do you know your name? How many children do you have? Are you hearing me?"

I heard him perfectly but, to my horror, I could do nothing to communicate. *Where is my robe? Where am I? What's happening! God, please help me!*

I tried to open my eyes. I had been given a number of medications, including morphine. The doctors became worried that I was over-medicated. When I was taken off the respirator, my metabolism sped up which increased the rate of the internal bleeding. Instead of waking up, I went into a rigid fetal position. The doctor suddenly became concerned and decided to treat my case as if I was having a major bleeding incident. He told my husband he was in fear that I was bleeding to death in front of his eyes. *God, let this be over soon! Was that awful headache a warning that something was about to happen? Why didn't I pay more attention to my headaches?*

To this day, I remember the horrible crunching sound of cartilage in my nose breaking as the tubes went in and out. Three trips to hell in one day.

Steven had a conversation with my private doctor whom I should have driven to see in the first place, instead of a chiropractor. The doctor advised him to instruct the hospital doctors to look in my brainstem for a possible stroke.

With a lawyer looking over their shoulders, the hospital doctors were afraid not to conduct the tests. Precious moments that meant so much to my recovery had been lost in a vain search to find a needle in a haystack. The latest medical technology was slipping beyond my reach. The medical miracles of the last twenty years were of no use for me. My youth and incredible physical shape worked against me in a sense, because it made the obvious hard to see.

The bill for the ER was over $96,000. For ninety-six grand, I was kept alive, but no one could figure out why I was sick.

The hospital where I was did not have an MRI (Magnetic Resonance Imaging) machine. If my private physician was right, the only way to know for sure if I was having a stroke was for me to have an MRI. I was therefore, transferred by ambulance to Torrance Memorial Hospital as quickly as arrangements could be made.

The ER doctor called the on-call neurologist, Dr. Kneisley, who took over my case. The transfer in the ambulance was a blur. I remember going in and out of consciousness. By the time I reached Torrance Memorial my body was in continuous convulsions. I vomited and was foaming at the mouth.

Where am I? What's happening? Suddenly, I found myself slowly moving into a machine. I could hear the voice of someone saying, "Try to lie still and relax. We have several sets of tests. Just try to lie still. In a moment, you'll be hearing some loud noises. It is okay." *Okay? I'm scared witless! What's happening to me?*

All of a sudden, I stopped moving. It was still. There was silence until slowly I heard what sounded like the beating of a drum, gradually getting louder and faster. Bang! Bang! Bang! I felt trapped and suffocating – claustrophobic. *I want out of here! I can't breathe.*

My body kept going into spasms, making it impossible to get a clear MRI reading. Everything after this was a blur. I remember nothing for what seemed a lifetime.

Many things would change, but there was one thing that remained constant: my husband, Steven. He would be the bridge between me and the world that existed outside my body. He would save my life.

I was admitted to the ICU for observation. Blue mittens were placed on my hands to prevent me from pulling any tube or IV out. Like I could pull anything out of anywhere with hands that won't move!

The following morning, I lay there staring up at the doctor and my husband. "It's hard to tell if she can understand us. I think she can hear us," the doctor said. *Yes! I can hear you. I can't move or speak, but I hear you. God, help me communicate somehow.*

From the Other Side of the Bed

*T*he doctors told me to get on the phone and start contacting funeral homes. They advised me to purchase a burial plot. They had no hope at this point for Kate's recovery.

They were realists. They had a lot of experience with strokes and since I had very little, they thought I was just being emotional and the sooner I was "realistic" the sooner I would start to heal. True, they had seen a lot of things, maybe even some "miracles," but miracles hardly ever happen. They were only doing what they thought was right to help me get on with my life and not suffer need-lessly.

I think there was more to it than that. From most doctors' viewpoints the worst thing that could happen to Kate was to live. They saw a young woman trapped inside her body, unable to interact with the outside world, living on and on for ten, twenty – maybe even fifty years in that awful condition. If there was a hell on earth surely it would be reserved for Kate Klugman.

I am sure they thought there must be another hell reserved for unrealistic, selfish, and foolish people like me who would not let her die.

Why should I accept their prognosis? The doctors had been wrong about me years before. Deep in my soul, I believed Kate was meant to live – and that she would live. Not only that, I had a deep personal conviction that life was meant to be lived – and lived in whatever circum-stances God intended. The doctors did not come out and say so, but they hinted and hinted around the idea that not only should I instruct them to not treat Kate – but that I *was delusional to have hope, and terribly irresponsible to try and keep her alive. It even got to the point where they thought I was a little – or a lot – crazy. More about that later.*

Please understand that at this point it was not a question of pulling the plug – that was a simpler moral issue (to them). What they wanted was to be allowed not to put the plug in, in the first place.

My husband refused to believe I was dying; but the doctor offered little hope. Dr. Kneisley, a neurologist, ordered some chest x-rays. I recall waking up and realizing I was lying on something flat, hard and cold. *What's happening now?*

Steven wanted some drugs administered to me that would lessen the swelling in my brain. "You must treat this as if she's had a stroke," he told the doctor. The neurologist refused, explaining he couldn't do that until they were sure what was wrong. Steven asked the doctor what would happen if I had a brain tumor and the doctor told him I would die within a few months. Once again he insisted that the doctor treat me for a stroke since by assuming that I had a stroke and not a tumor, some good could be done. The doctor refused my husband's request and a day passed before the anti-inflammatory treatment was administered.

The doctor recommended and ordered an emergency vertebral angiogram to determine if I had a brain tumor or a stroke. This had both prognostic and therapeutic implications. Because I had previously been given blood thinners, the procedure was touch-and-go. I was given a shot of Vitamin K to help speed up the clotting of my blood.

Dr. Jeffrey Saver's Comments:

*S*troke *is injury to the brain due to blockage or rupture of a blood vessel. The brain requires a constant flow of blood to carry oxygen and nutrients to nerve cells. Four main arteries carry* blood to the brain: the right and left carotid arteries and the right and left vertebral arteries. In Kate's case – damage to nerve tracks passing through the brain-stem disconnected the upper parts of the brain, the cerebral hemispheres, from the spinal cord and the body. Kate became "locked in" – her intact cerebral hemispheres enabling her to be awake and aware, but unable to move her limbs or facial muscles because the connections between the cerebral hemispheres to the spinal cord were injured by the stroke.

Stroke is the third leading cause of death and the leading cause of disability in the developed world. Stroke is often thought of as a disease of the elderly. However, strokes do commonly affect middle-aged adults, young adults, and even children. Up to one third of all strokes occur in individuals under the age of 65. "Locked-in Syndrome" is one of the rarest and most feared consequences of a stroke.

From the Other Side of the Bed

*T*he Hippocratic Oath says to "first do no harm." Well you can't do much harm to someone you consider pretty much dead already, so it made sense to me that if they figured they could do no harm, then they should try to do some good.

My logic was simple. I wanted Kate treated for a stroke since treating a stroke could be beneficial – and would do no harm. I did not want her treated for a brain tumor since treating a brain tumor made no difference. To this day, I do not know why I was not listened to. Would it have made a difference if the doctors had listened to me? I will never know. In retrospect it is a question I should never have had to ask.

I was the responsible decision maker, however, I was being ignored. I commanded, I begged, I pleaded, but I could not get the medical beast to move. Why the doctors *were so committed to death was something I still don't understand. We had a very good doctor but we wound up at a hospital where our doctor did not have admitting privileges. Kate's outcome could have been quite different if I had been working with our doctor from the start.*

Regardless of who you are working with, don't ever assume the doctors know everything. They are intelligent and well educated but they don't know the patient as well as you do. Make your voice heard. Be kind but be firm. If you can't do both – be firm! Do what you know is right for the patient. I knew Kate. I was her husband. I was her best friend. I knew she was a fighter and I knew she wanted to live. Was I taking a risk in that assumption? Yes. As it turned out, I was right. Besides, I had taken the question to God.

I was wheeled into the operating room on a gurney with my husband at my side. The procedure was too much for Steven and he passed out (protective as ever, he tried his best to fall away from the . operating table).

Now I was alone. Everything was stainless steel and clean looking. How eerie. Dr. Hoffman, a radiologist performed the angiogram. I don't remember much. I recall the surgeon leaning over and saying, "Great news, Kate. You've suffered a stroke." *Great news for who?* "We found the problem. Your vertebral artery is occluded." *What is he saying? What is a stroke? What does occluded mean? How is this good news?*

Doubt had been replaced with hope – or had it? Since my husband had fainted in the operating room, he didn't meet Dr. Hoffman. Fate placed the doctor in the elevator as Steven was riding up to my room. He heard Dr. Hoffman telling a nurse that I was the worst thing he had seen in a very long time. He said I was a tragic case and could look forward to death if I were lucky and could look forward to life if I were not lucky. My husband kept this in his heart and filed it away under mistaken beliefs that would be overcome by a gracious God.

From the Other Side of the Bed

K̶ate seemed to want me in sight at all times. I sensed she felt if I was there everything would be alright. That prompted me to go into the operating room with her when she had her angiogram. I would have been a doctor – if I could tolerate blood.

It was just too much for me. I fainted. I did have the presence of mind to fall outward (how thoughtful of me) and so did not contaminate the operating field.

Because I fainted quite early in the process, Dr. Hoffman had never met me, so afterwards in the elevator he had no idea who I was. No doubt he would never have said such a thing to the husband of his patient. Dr. Hoffman's opinion that Kate would be better off dead was not a shining ray of hope; it was another piece in a puzzle that I felt only God could solve.

Overnight, my life had been turned into a nightmare. The doctor started me on the anticoagulation drug, heparin. Although I was breathing spontaneously, I was unable to handle my secretions and remained intubated. I was watched very closely.

Another doctor came by for a consultation. She felt I needed a feeding tube placed in my stomach because of the difficulty of getting enough nourishment from my IVs. I was too sick and frail to be moved to the operating room. A nurse put a mouth guard in for me to bite on. *Why is she doing that? What are they doing?* Suddenly, it dawned on me. The doctor thought I was comatose and they did not give me adequate pain medication. Imagine being cut into and not being able to respond? I could feel my silent screams echoing inside my head. *Oh no! Stop! Please, God! Wait! I'm awake!*

The doctor was already operating on me to put the tube in. I felt her cutting my stomach open. I felt everything – the entire operation – every cut – and I had no way of communicating. The operation lasted an eternity.

This tube was where I would receive all my nourishment and medications. From this point on, all medications were crushed up, dissolved with a little water before being put into a syringe and passed through the tube. How had I lived through that? How could anyone live through it?

From the Other Side of the Bed.

*W*hen you're as sick and paralyzed as Kate was, your bowel movements become a matter of life and death. One of the first things I would ask each morning was, "Did Kate have a bowel movement?"

At first things went fine, but then everything went bad – worse than bad. Kate's digestive system crashed. Her intestinal tract became impacted. The GI specialist who had placed the G-tube in Kate's stomach was called back. I remember meeting her before the surgery. She was not exactly Merry Sunshine. She referred to Kate as "this unfortunate woman," and was very pessimistic about Kate's chances. I got the idea that she felt her talents were being wasted on someone who was pretty much dead already.

Now she was back in front of this "most unfortunate woman," and the only thing she could do was add to Kate's pain. To resolve the problem of the impacted bowel, her feeding tube had to be turned off. Now we were going to add to her misery by depriving her of food.

It's very hard to keep accurate track of time when you're in ICU. A day is a year and week is a decade. The best recollection that Kate and I have is that Kate's tube was turned off for eight days. I can't swear to the exact number of days, but I can swear it was an eternity. Each day and each night I would ask the same question, "Can she be fed now? Can she be fed?" The answer would be the same. "No, she cannot, may not and will not."

This ordeal would touch Kate more than any other part of her sickness, because you don't find too many people, if any, who live to tell you about what it's like to go without food – involuntarily – for so many days. Most people in that condition die and therefore, have little to report.

It was this experience that drew us to the Terri Schiavo case. Terry could not speak for herself. At the time of her adventure in starvation, Kate could not speak for herself either. When the Schiavo case hit the press, Kate could speak – and speak she did.

Whatever you may think about what happened to Terri, you cannot deny Kate's experience was real, personal and horribly painful. You, the reader can make of it whatever you will, but one thing cannot be denied – it was a horrifying, hellish experience for Kate, and who really knows what Terri felt before she died.

Dr. Kolodney, a lung specialist, was called in to monitor my breathing problems which had become severe. He was the first doctor to believe in my chances of recovery. He was the only one who would listen to Steven. At this point, other doctors thought Steven was insane because he refused to give up. They even noted in my medical records that Steven was delusional because he refused to believe that I would die.

From the Other Side of the Bed

I was dumfounded, confused, and scared. I was 48 years old with two children on my hands – a three-year-old and an 18- month-old. Though I was a modern father and had changed a lot of diapers (Kate would argue about that, but these are my comments – not hers!), I certainly was not a domestic god (Kate would not argue with that!). I was not a housekeeper. It wasn't beneath me, it was above me. I had no idea how to run a house. The kids were in real danger of starving to death if I was in charge of preparing their meals.

I had married a much younger woman; a woman whom I thought would outlive me by years, and now here she was, dying in front of my eyes – of "natural causes." It was more than I could bear, yet, what could I do? I wasn't a doctor – so I could do nothing, Right? Wrong! I was a devoted father with a wife that I loved and wanted to save. I was also a lawyer with fundamental beliefs about the sacredness of life and a fundamental attitude about people getting in my way of doing what I felt was right – and legal.

The doctors took me out into the hall and they had "the death talk" with me. "Be realistic Mr. Klugman," they told me, "sometimes life is not worth preserving. If Kate survives this stroke she is going to likely be locked in."

The idea was horrifying. Kate was healthy in every way and could wind up living 50 years locked in a living hell. It would be just like being sealed in a glass coffin. She would be able to feel everything but she would not be able to move any part of her body.

The doctors told me that if I truly cared for my wife, I would do what was best for Kate – not for me – and would let her go.

As I pondered all that was happening, a bit of Dylan Thomas I once read in college kept running through my head. "Do not go gentle into that good night. Rage, rage against the dying of the light…"

That seemed right to me. I was not willing for Kate to go into the good night, gently or not. More importantly, I was convinced that she would not want to give up so easily either.

Life is much too precious to just give up without a fight. Maybe, just maybe, a time would come that we would "let her go," but not now – not yet.

I told the doctor that I would watch everything that everyone did, and I would not forgive anyone who did less than their best to save my wife. I went out and bought a clip board and started carrying it around with me. I never wrote anything on it, I wanted the doctors to think I was watching and documenting. I demanded their best – and would settle for no less.

To his everlasting credit, Dr. Kolodney took the time to speak with Steven – and listen to him. After some initial rough going, they became willing partners to see that I would survive this awful stroke. Dr. Kolodney's compassion, skill and belief made all the difference in the world. Without the help of a lawyer and a doctor working together, there is no doubt in my mind that I would have fulfilled the expectations of the medical staff and died within days – or worse, been locked in for the rest of my life.

I was not done with tubes, not by a long shot. My husband asked Dr. Kolodney to remove the tube down my airway. This was truly an amazing suggestion. Steven was trying to prevent me from having a scar. He had convinced the doctor that my position was not hopeless. The doctor agreed, but his nurse begged him not to. She felt I was desperately ill and that I would drown in my own secretions if they took the tubes out.

She was right. As soon as the tubes were removed, I began to go down hill. I could not handle my secretions. I could not breathe on my own. I was rapidly drowning in my own saliva. My oxygen saturation level began to fall, requiring constant suctioning. Dr. Kolodney told Steven that I needed an emergency tracheotomy. "This will be a tiny, two-inch scar; it is a matter of life and death," he stated.

Approval was given and a tracheotomy was performed July 5th. Looking back, it seems insane that the biggest worry on my caregiver's mind was my having a tiny scar, but it was evidence that they believed I would be a normal woman again.

From the Other Side of the Bed

One of the craziest things I did was to try and keep Kate from having a tracheotomy. At this moment, when Kate's life hung in the balance, I had a good deal of my attention on her vanity. Kate is an extraordinary beauty. I knew how much pride she took in her appearance and I wanted to keep her from having a scar.

I did learn a powerful lesson through this experience though. I learned to trust the nursing staff. Dr. Kolodney and I both thought Kate would be fine; her nurse knew better. I came to realize how little time the doctors spend with a patient as compared to a nurse. When I wanted to get something done, I learned to enlist the nurses. I also learned to say the heck with vanity!

At this point I was a little naïve about what it would take for Kate to recover. I believed that she would fully recover and be normal in every way. I don't regret feeling that way. I think one always hopes for the best and tries for the best. Sometimes it is even helpful not to fully understand the price of something. It's much better to focus on its value than on its price.

As horrible as the breathing tubes down my nose had been, I had little comfort from the tracheotomy. I was producing an overabundance of fluids. A vacuum device was inserted into the trachea to keep my lungs clear. Every time a respiratory therapist approached me, my body tightened into convulsions. If I could have been able to move, I would have jumped off the bed as they began sucking the mucus out of my lungs. The treatments were unbearable. *Here we go again. How can anyone put up with this?*

I can still feel the suction treatments that kept my airway open and my lungs from filling up with fluid. I would recover emotionally from this ordeal, only for it to begin again. At this point in my recovery, I needed the treatments every twenty minutes.

I was not being given pain medication because of the collateral neurological problems. I had to tough it out through pain, isolation and extreme boredom – and my friend, the darkness.

Life in ICU was constant, unchanging, with little hope. The days dragged on and on. Seventy days would pass before I'd leave the ICU. I heard nothing but the constant beeping of the machines keeping me alive. I could sense the feeding tube dangling from my stomach with no way of reaching down to adjust it. The memories of those circumstances and procedures haunt me still.

I was in the prime of my life, yet I had suffered a massive stroke. How was that possible? I was completely paralyzed except for some involuntary eye movements. I was conscious, had unfettered cognitive thinking abilities, but was unable to speak or move. I had a perfect sense of pain. I hurt everywhere but I could move nowhere.

Why should I live? How can this be called living? Why should I take my next breath? I don't want to leave my children, whatever pain may come, whatever horror is around the corner, I will endure whatever treatment, no matter how dehumanizing. I have to overcome any obstacle to get back to my children. Home. I want to go home.

I am in darkness, but the darkness is not empty. There is a strong presence here. God was with me, so I could not be without hope. I was trapped inside my body. Steven was outside, doing everything – moving heaven and hell to reach me.

From the Other Side of the Bed

I remember when the doctors said Kate would not live through the night. I wondered if maybe they were right. I did not believe them. I really had no reason to distrust them. I did not know what to do. I decided to go into her room to say goodbye to my Kate. Maybe she wasn't there, maybe she was dead already. I walked into her room.

Death was everywhere; it was such a strong presence that I could reach out and touch it.

Suddenly, the irrepressible urge to pray came over me. I dropped to my knees beside Kate's bed and prayed as only the hopeless and desperately broken-hearted can pray. I didn't care who heard me. This was between me and God.

I prayed for what seemed an eternity. Sometimes I spoke silently, sometimes out loud in words. Mostly it was my broken heart crying out to my God; a God I believed cared for me and loved Kate.

I knew of another empty tomb and had faith that Jesus opened his tomb for us all – and would open Kate's tomb and let her come back to me. And for that I pleaded as only a child can, for something that means everything.

A bright light came into the room. It lit my face and my body brighter than the sun. Doctors will tell you that people see what they want to see. They say that hope and emotion play tricks on the mind. You might say that perhaps the strain was just so bad, the pain so awful, that I willed my eyes to see things that were not there. I do know this, and so do you, Kate did not die that night or the next or the next. I am telling you that from that moment on, there was no death in the room. Kate was not dying anymore. It would be some time before I could convince the doctors that I was not crazy. Now everyone knows that, crazy though I may have been, I was right.

Before this experience in prayer, I was not sure that I was doing the right thing to force the doctors to do every-thing possible to save Kate. I now had my answer; as any trial attorney would do I moved forward with conviction, regardless of what anyone else might have said, especially the opposition, to try and convince me that I was wrong.

When I came out of the room I found Kate's treating physician and told him – in my own sweet and charming way – that I had received an answer to a prayer and that Kate was alive and could get better and that I expected him to do everything possible.

The doctor looked at me like I was delusional, but I have ceased long ago to worry too much about what others think of me or my mental state. I told the doctor that I was a malpractice attorney, which I am not, and would be looking over everyone's shoulders. I made it clear that if my wife died, a lawsuit would be filed. Did my threats help or hurt Kate's cause? I don't know, but it surely got everyone's attention.

Even with my kind and gentle attitude, I still had problems with the medical staff. I wanted them to treat Kate for a stroke (remember, at this point, they still didn't know what exactly had happened with her).

They did not do as I wished. Early in the game, her neurologist had refused to give her heparin until he could confirm that she did not have a brain tumor. I pleaded and pleaded but to no avail. They refused to act until they had a chance to do an angiogram.

I have always been haunted by the thought that the time wasted, more than a full day, may have made the difference between a full recovery and the recovery Kate was able to obtain – as amazing as it is. I will never know. I do know that this first confrontation convinced me that pleading was not my strongest skill – threatening was more my style and from then on it was the hit them first with the 2x4 to get their attention strategy, then diplomacy. That seemed to work.

In his efforts to move heaven and hell, Steven got some help in moving heaven. He made some calls and within hours it began, a dozen people praying for me. By week's end, thousands of people around the world were praying for me around the clock. Not an hour, not a minute went by that someone, somewhere, was not praying for me. I could not see help, but I could feel it approach. I had my faith, my husband and my children and now a thousand angels beating on the doors of heaven on my behalf.

~

Prayer journal excerpts while Kate was in ICU:

Dear Kate and Steven, I am moved by Christ's love for you both and so thankful for your lives crossing my path. Surely He took up our infirmities – "and by His stripes we are healed." (Isaiah 53:5.5-6.) By His wounds, Kate is healed, because of those dark hours two thousands years ago, I pray God will honor His word and heal you day by day. I love you so much, Kate and look forward to seeing all the wonderful things God has planned for you. Love, Karen Johnson

~

Kate, In Mark 5:34 Jesus said, "Daughter, your faith has made you well. Go in peace and be healed..." I thank God for you and pray that while God is healing you, your peace is mighty. You are in my prayers. I love you, Chris Kirby

~

Dear Kate, It's exciting to know He is healing you. Sunday at church my daughter Christina and I passed Stephanie being carried up the stairs. I didn't even realize who it was until I felt a little arm reach out and touch me. She recognized me, and certainly wanted us to know she was there. Stephanie's a special girl and God is going to give you many more years to enjoy your daughters. Love, Laura Warfield

~

My Dearest Friend Kate, I miss you! You are in my heart and in my prayers. I love you. You have been such a blessing in my life. You will be out of here soon. We will see you through. How strong you are. May God heal you quickly, Cherri

~

Kate, My beautiful sister in Christ. I'm touched by the impact you have had on many lives. People have been drawn closer to Christ and have been blessed because of you – He loves you with a love so great we cannot fully understand. I love you. Juli

~

Dear Kate, I love you. This is temporary. I am so excited about seeing you stand up in church and giving your testimony. God is going to get the glory out of this. You are going to be stronger, happier, more blessed and closer to Jesus than you have ever been. You will be well soon, and very soon! By Jesus Christ's stripes, you are healed. Love, Debbie Albino

~

Dearest Kate, You are doing so very well – major improvements every day. Now you are slightly moving your right hand and foot and starting your left side. You are a strong woman, physically and spiritually, keep fighting. "Our God is an awesome God, he reigns with power and love..." Love, Penny

~

Dear Kate, Thanks for letting me play the violin for you tonight. You are a fighter! Keep working that physical therapy, max the stair master! Still the thoughts, listen for God's voice. Resist the enemy's lies, learn what He wants you to know right now. You'll be fine and I'm praying for you. Love, Lisa Anders

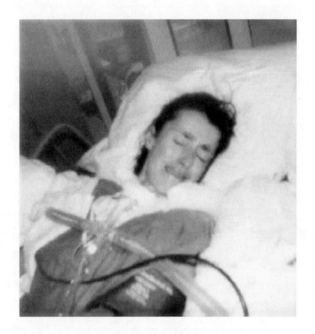

Kate, in ICU

Chapter Three

~

Blink Once for "Yes"

I felt very frightened and isolated. Although there was a steady flow of visitors – familiar faces of friends popping in and out of ICU – I was alone, still unable to communicate with anyone in any way.

I felt like a character in a Twilight Zone episode. There were moments I doubted my sanity. Sometimes I wished this wasn't real, it was all in my imagination – a bad dream – because then I could recover and this dreadful play would be over. The director would shout "cut," the camera would stop rolling, and I could get up and go home. What a lovely thought. But I knew something much worse had happened to me than just losing my mind. My mind bounced back and forth, like a ping-pong ball between pain, loneliness and terror. I knew my only companion was God, the only one I could communicate with.

No kind and loving God would let this happen. If I could just tell someone I am alive, then I could get help. No matter how hard I tried, I couldn't speak. I tried to mouth the word home to anyone who came near. *Don't any of you understand me? I have to be able to get home; this has to be a bad dream.*

Sadly, I wasn't going anywhere physically or spiritually. I was attached to the wall by wires, attached to machines with IVs and tubes through a hole in my throat and hanging from my stomach.

Close the hole in my neck and stomach, remove the tubes; I am outta here. But I am dead. I can't leave because I am tied to this earth by tubes and wires. It's no use. My cries for help are useless! Who can I cry to? Who will hear me? I can't even cry. No real tears flow and no sound comes out.

I noticed everything. I noticed nothing. I just wanted to go home. Steven and a friend, Rhonda, were in my room discussing concerns about my 18-month old, Rachel who was fighting an ear infection. Steven was trying to remember where we kept Rachel's medicine so he could tell our housekeeper.

I should be handling this. I wish I could speak right now. How can such a simple thing like speaking be so impossible?

Steven is always talking to her or the kids – or one of his fellow attorneys – but never to me. *Oh, for Pete's sake, Steven, it's where it's always been – in the refrigerator right next to.... That man, I swear; he would lose his head if it wasn't stitched on.*

Steven – Steven! STEVEN! Oh, what's the use, I can't speak. I can't do a damn thing but think. I want to TALK. If I could just tell people what is going on.

Wait! Steven is talking to me. Do I know where it is? Steven, for Pete's sake, for a smart lawyer, you can be awfully dumb. Of course, I know where it is but you know I can't talk. What? Can I blink my eyes? I don't know – I'll try.

"Kate you did it! I know you did it on purpose, right?" Steven was thrilled over one stupid blink. "Come on do it again. Kate, you can do it. Just blink. Your life may depend on it. You can do it," Steven pleaded. "Blink once for 'yes' and twice for 'no'."

Blink once for "yes" and twice for "no"? This is exhausting.

From the Other Side of the Bed

I knew this was going to work out, I just did. I had this sense that I was in a movie and I knew the script. I was going to ask Kate to blink and she would. I swear that I had seen that somewhere in a movie. I was not surprised when Kate blinked back. I was expecting even a little bit more. She was going to blink and then jump up and dance the tarantella.

The moment was unreal to me when she first blinked. It had this surrealistic quality. It was as though I was watching what was happening from a great distance. I was excited, yes, but also strangely detached. I felt, "Okay, now we got it going, let's keep it moving and soon we'll be out of here."

I knew that now I could convince people that Kate was a person. I could start to get her all the things that "real" people get. When Kate was a "vegetable" she had very few options, but now that she was a person, there was a world of opportunity open to me.

Of course it wasn't that easy, it never is. No one was going to give her anything unless I fought for it. The economics of the thing made it emotionally and financially easier for them to think of Kate as a vegetable. I knew what I would have to do, which was to demand again and again that no one be allowed to discuss anything short of a full recovery.

No one agreed with me at this point, but I had enough going to create some belief that I was right and the doctors were wrong. Belief can be a powerful tool in the right hands.

Now I could do two things. I could think. I could blink.
In a blink, my life changed.
In a blink, I was a person again.
"Praise God! Praise God!" Steven said.
Praise God is right. Thank you, God. Thank you, Steven. You knew I could do it, even when I didn't. I have made contact. First contact! I am not alone in the universe!

Not wanting Steven to be heart broken, Rhonda suggested the blink was a coincidence. "No Rhonda, I refuse to believe that.

Okay, Kate, do it again. Blink once for 'yes'," he said watching me intently.

This was it; my whole life hinged on this one chance. *Can I blink my eyelids because I want to? I'm not sure I can do this again.* It felt like a million years had gone by and everything I had tried to do – every time I tried to move something, say something, do something – I had failed.

I asked God to help me. I thought and concentrated hard. Nothing happened. Was it a coincidence? I wanted so much to believe I could do this.

"Come on Kate. You can do it," Steven said.

It's no use. I just can't. I gave up – and suddenly, I blinked.

I blinked! I did it! Thank you, God.

"Now, Kate, try blinking twice for 'no'," he said unconsciously holding his hands to his mouth in anticipation.

This takes a lot of energy. I hope I can do this. Slowly, I blinked – twice. *Dear God, I did it! You did it. We did it. I can blink. I can communicate.*

Like a little boy, Steven ran for the nurses' station, then skidded to a stop and ran back to me. He hollered "Praise God!" and ran back to the nurses' station. "I want this documented. Kate can communicate! I want a sign made so people know she understands – can understand – does understand. Make a sign that says, 'Kate is alive and she understands.'"

Steven is not E. F. Hutton but when he speaks, people listen. Still, no one moved fast enough for him. No one could. So he grabbed some paper and a big green marker and made his own sign. He hung it over the bed. In large handwritten letters it said:

THIS IS A HUMAN BEING LYING HERE.
SHE UNDERSTANDS WHAT YOU SAY.
PLEASE TREAT HER AS A PERSON.

Praise God? Praise God is right! Thank you, God. I've made contact. Now I am not alone.

From the Other Side of the Bed

*I*t was my job to get people to agree that Kate was going to get better. We all agree to a lot of things; and when we agree, we give things power.

Everything I did was calculated. I thought about how I was going to help her get better. I thought about it twenty four hours a day. I was always looking for what I could do to enhance her chance for full recovery. To do that I needed to get people, the hospital staff in particular, to agree with me that Kate was going to be a miracle.

When you are going to be a miracle people do extra things for you. When Kate was fighting an infection, the staff tested her every few hours instead of once a day. They did that because at one point in time, the entire hospital was rooting for a miracle. The first step in getting people on our side was to put the sign up over Kate's bed that read "This is a human being ..." Maybe it should have said, "Kate is a miracle ..."

Starting that day, I communicated by blinking my eyes. My life had been saved. I wasn't quite grateful enough. They had kept me alive, but so far had done little to help me live. Until now, they assumed I was permanently and totally paralyzed, and essentially brain dead, so I wasn't receiving therapy, it was a waste of money. Now, I could prove them wrong. *I can open and close my eyes on purpose. I can communicate. I am alive. I am real. I deserve to live – not just exist!*

The process was exhausting, but I had no other way of communicating with the outside world. The nurses gave my husband a clipboard with a sheet of the alphabet attached.

My blink-language became more complex. I would blink "yes" or "no" to each letter as Steven pointed to them.

Realizing that because I had only heard bits and pieces of my diagnosis and prognosis (Diagnosis: total paralysis. Prognosis:

imminent or, at best, eventual death) he said, "Kate, do you really understand what has happened to you?"

I blinked "No." Steven said, "You have had a stroke." I didn't blink, I just stared at him. *What's that?*

He read my mind. Grabbing a piece of paper and pencil he drew a diagram, explaining what had happened. *Steven, I'm too sick to be looking at diagrams.* I listened to him ramble on. *I don't have a clue what you are saying.*

From that point on, everyone used the alphabet board. It took effort to figure out what I was trying to say. Communicating to form the words was slow and tiresome. I struggled to keep blinking long enough to spell words. *How can this be so hard? I can't even do this simple thing.*

A pencil was used to point to each row of letters. I blinked if the letter I wanted was in that row, and blinked again when they came to the letter I wanted. Simple, but it worked. Trying to express myself in this way was incredibly time consuming, but it was all I had. Just to say "I love you" required 16 blinks. At this point, I was so weak that I had only about a twenty-blink vocabulary. *This is frustrating! There has to be an easier way.*

During my ICU stay there were heated exchanges between the doctors and Steven. The doctors, though now accepting the fact of my survival, offered little hope of actual recovery. They based their prognosis on statistics. Steven based his on stubbornness. They wanted Steven to be more realistic. He wanted them to be more positive.

Statistically, I had one chance in a million to live. Even though they knew I could hear and respond, many people still treated me as if I was already dead. *Why are people talking in front of me as if I'm not here? I can hear and understand everything they are saying.* It was like listening in on a party line while the neighbors gossip about you, and planned your funeral.

Later, I learned from Steven that he had to vigilantly maintain the position that I would recover. If he let go of the idea for one moment, one second, I was a dead woman. My chances were one in a million. To realize my one chance, someone was going to have to spend one million dollars. The doctors didn't want to spend that kind of money on me, nor did the hospital or the insurance company. It was like buying a million one dollar tickets to win a million dollar lottery – with no guarantees.

To be fair, it wasn't just the money, honestly, the prognosis was terrible. The doctors told Steven if my life were saved I would be nothing more than a vegetable. It would be better if I died. Because I was otherwise young, strong and healthy, I could live years hooked up to tubes, unable to talk or move and awake most of the time. I would feel pain but be locked into my body. It was a horrifying prognosis.

Steven refused to believe this. No matter how bleak things got, his faith kept him going. The staff mistook his constant prayers for a delusion in which Steven thought he was talking directly to God. (Well, actually, he was talking to God, it is called prayer.)

From the Other Side of the Bed

*K*ate and I both feel that her recovery was a miracle. So do a number of medical experts who saw what happened to her. We believe that her recovery is an example of answered prayer.

This is supposed to be a Christian nation, right? Christianity accepts the concept of prayer. So why is it so crazy for us to believe we can talk to God?

When people talk about prayer they often become uncomfortable. We have all heard people say God always answers prayer, sometimes He just says, "No." I have even seen a recent study of a few hundred people that proves that prayer does not work. You would have a hard time convincing Kate, me or the thousands who prayed for her, that such a "study" had any validity whatsoever.

In some ways it is amusing that the doctors thought I was delusional or fanatic when I was talking to God as if

He actually heard me; and that I fully expected my prayers to be answered.

Don't get me wrong, I have no notion that God is a cosmic bell boy who goes around answering prayer on demand. There are people who think that if you really do believe hard enough that you will have your prayer answered; strangely, I am not really one of them. If that were the case, we would be God's boss, and not His children.

I am also convinced that my answered prayer had nothing to do with my character or good deeds. Our prayers are not answered because Kate and I are special, they are answered because God is special.

If anyone has the idea that I was some kind of pious prayer warrior, I humbly admit that I was not, and am not, a person with a deep or extraordinary prayer life. I find it hard to pray. I mumble something, then look up and cock my ear and listen; but mainly the sky is empty and nothing comes.

It was not like that in 1995, though. The sky did open and I could hear and I could see. I was praying with an intensity that was almost superhuman, groaning with utterance that words could not describe. I was clear in what I wanted; I was moved to prayer by the sheer help-lessness and desperation of this situation. There was nothing I could do that was going to matter one bit. Sure, I had lots of things I could do and I did do, but none of them – absent the miracle of God's grace – was going to accomplish a thing.

I was 48 years old and about to be a widower and a single parent of two toddlers. I was terrified. I was heart-broken. I was in the deepest of despair. So what, after all, did I have left to do? What else could I do? I could only pray.

I guess it is like the old saying, "There are no atheists in foxholes." This was war. This was a life and death fight.

There is something in the human heart that calls out from the darkness to the light. Some have a lot of faith in those circumstances, some a little. At those moments, the moments when your wife is lying there, dying a horrible death before your eyes, any little bit of faith seems enough to cry out to a God without hesitation or question. And that is what I did.

As I prayed, I sensed something. I could not prove I was not crazy as the doctors thought, but if we know a tree by its fruit, then I guess I was not crazy. I was offered a gift. God let me know that each and every day I would see something hopeful – and I did. Sometimes it was a big thing, like seeing Kate blink "yes" or "no" to my questions or seeing a finger move a thousandth of an inch. Sometimes it was a little thing, like a doctor saying, "I cannot explain why, but I think your wife is going to get better." I never did have a day where I could not find that one hopeful thing to dream about when I went to bed that night.

It could all be just a coincidence, and the wise people of this world are going to read this and say to themselves that everything I saw, heard and felt was either a coincidence or an invention of my own mind. It could be they are right, but Kate and I went for a walk today, so you explain it.

Making matters worse (or better), within hours of my stroke, the waiting room was filled with fellow church people. At times, there were forty or more people in the waiting room. They prayed. They sang. They brought potluck dinners to the hospital. The smell of antiseptic and tuna casserole still lingers in my brain.

Steven was free to be at the hospital because friends were at our house around the clock, day in and day out. Every afternoon and night, a different person would cook for my family.

The waiting room was never empty. A schedule was worked out to guarantee that someone was at the hospital twenty-four hours a day. I was totally and completely helpless. The people watching over me were a great comfort and blessing.

Dr. Jeffrey Saver's Comments:

*P*atients in the locked-in state are awake and aware but unable to move their limbs or most facial muscles to signal their responsiveness. They do generally retain their ability to blink and to move the eyes up and down. The neural circuitry controlling blinking and vertical gaze resides in the highest portion of the brainstem. This region is usually spared from injuries affecting the rest of the brainstem. As a result, patients can use blinking to communicate. A variety of coding systems have been developed to facilitate communication with the locked-in patient, but even the most sophisticated is frustrating and exhausting to employ. Success requires, as Kate exhibited, a determined and resilient spirit.

Chapter Four

~

The Cavalry

T rying not to startle me, a woman leaned over and gently touched my hand. "Kate, my name is Betsy and I'm from Physical Therapy. How are you this morning?"

She paused to see if I could comprehend her words. In her silver rimmed glasses and white medical lab coat, Betsy looked like an angel. I knew I wasn't dead. I wasn't even asleep. Those machines made sure of that.

A petite middle-aged woman with auburn hair, Betsy was the first therapist to work with me. Every moment she was with me gave me hope. She used terms I had never heard. I liked it because this meant she knew I was in there. To me, Betsy was walking, living, breathing hope. *How am I? I'd be fine if I wasn't here!*

Betsy said, "I'll be working with your lower body."

What's wrong with my body? I know I had something called a stroke. I still don't understand why I can't move. If only I could say something out loud then maybe I could get my questions answered.

I hadn't yet learned that I could blink. I had lots of questions and no way of communicating.

As she was leaning over me, a tiny gold pin in the shape of an ice skate boot caught my eye. It was attached to the lapel of her jacket. *She ice skates?*

Betsy's voice was soothing and gentle, and I could see she was passionate about her work. She was also compassionate with her patients.

Steven and a friend were in my room one morning when a cheerful Betsy came in with her assistant. *Who is he? Is he helping her?* In his late twenties, Ron was tan and muscular. He looked like he could be a lifeguard on the beach rather than working in a hospital. *I may be sick but you're awfully cute!* I was embarrassed to have him help.

I soon learned that Ron was Betsy's hands. Ron provided the physical strength Betsy needed. "We think you might be strong enough to try and sit up on the edge of the bed," she said standing beside Ron. What they meant was that I would be strong enough to be held up by Ron without passing out. "Don't worry Kate, we are here to help you," she said. Betsy wheeled a stool over to the edge of the bed. "Okay Ron, let's begin to sit her up."

My bed was equipped with a special air-mattress that helped prevent bedsores. Ron turned the switch off, deflating the mattress. *I'm sinking. I am disappearing!* "Careful Ron, make sure the lines aren't pulling," she instructed.

Hey, wait, is my gown open? I was beginning to realize that modesty had no meaning in this world of the sick and dying. With many maneuvers and attempts, I found myself sitting on the edge of the bed. Ron's strong arms held my frail body. I felt dizzy; everything around me spinning. *I don't like this! I want to lie down again. I am not strong enough to sit up. This is so painful.*

"Wow! Look at you, how does that feel?" Betsy said elated. *It feels weird, I prefer being back in bed.* "Pick your head up, keep it up Kate," she said. *I'm trying. I'm trying! My head feels like lead. The only thing that feels good is leaning on Ron's chest.* "Hold it up Kate, don't let your head droop," said Betsy repeating herself. "Do you feel lightheaded or dizzy?" she asked. *I feel like my head is going to drop off.*

After what felt like an eternity, I was sitting up somewhat, with assistance. "How's that Kate; you're sitting up!" Betsy said.

"Good job Kate!" Ron cheered. *I feel weak and sick. Please let me lie down.*

"Ron, keep holding onto Kate," she said.

My friend Rhonda reached into her handbag and took out a compact mirror. "Here Betsy, I have a small mirror for Kate to look at herself." *Is she nuts? I don't want to look at myself.* Betsy held the mirror up. "There Kate, you can take a look at yourself." Luckily for me the mirror tilted and all I could see was the ceiling.

Gradually, my body started to sway backward. I had no control of my torso. My mouth was closed tight and my head went back into its locked position to the right side. *I need desperately to lie down. I can't sit here anymore. I am exhausted.*

Everyone was ecstatic. I was tired. Steven was thrilled. "Wow Betsy, it's amazing to see her sitting up like that."

I was relieved to lie down. The Cavalry kept coming – the PTs, OTs and a Speech Pathologist named Carolyn. She gave me a warm smile when she introduced herself. "Kate, I'm Carolyn from the Speech Pathology Department. How are you today?" *How am I? Miserable! I want out of here! I just want to go home.* "Can you try to touch the corners of your mouth with your tongue?"

"Yes, Kate can do that," Steven said. "Betsy has given us a sheet with simple mouth exercises. I have Kate do those every hour." *Yeah, he doesn't let me forget!*

From the Other Side of the Bed

I am not very strict. Ask my daughters. Those who know me would not call me disciplined or a disciplinarian. Though that was okay for me, it was not going to work in this situation. I had this deep conviction that if Kate was going to get better, I was going to have to be disciplined, and a disciplinarian. More than that, I was going to have to be ruthless. I didn't like the idea, but I knew it was a matter of life or no life.

I modeled myself after the drill sergeant in "An Officer and a Gentleman." No matter how many repetitions Kate did, I wanted one more and then another. I knew that, unlike me, Kate was amazingly disciplined. She was an athlete; she was the queen of the work-out room. I knew she knew how to work out, so I used that to motivate her.

All those months and years in the gym would now pay off. Kate was able to reach down inside and apply herself to her therapy more than any one could imagine. It was awesome. It was truly inspirational. The medical staff and the patients were moved by what they saw; and therefore, they tried harder to help by giving her a little more attention and a little extra encouragement.

Now it was starting to look to everyone like we were in the midst of a miracle and everyone wanted a part in it. As I mentioned before, I had that thought earlier in her recovery and now it was paying off – big time!

"Good. Okay Kate, try to imitate me as I do some oral motor commands," Carolyn said. I followed her directions, finding it hard to control my secretions. By now I had learned my blink-language, so I blinked "yes" or "no" to her simple questions. *I can understand everything you say.*

These exercises are so primitive you could teach them to a monkey. Here I am a grown woman and I can't even move my body. I can't talk or swallow and, for some reason, you are having me stick my tongue out. How can that help me speak? Steven kept at me hour after hour. *I hate his nagging, but I'm in no shape to fight him or anyone else.*

Carolyn turned to my husband, "What I'd like to try is attaching a Passy-Muir valve to her trachea tube. Kate is a good candidate for this. It will help her relearn to speak." *I'd love to be able to speak.*

"Wonderful. What is a Passy-Muir valve?" Steven asked.

"It's a speaking valve. It allows her to control the air in her trachea so she can speak," she said.

Carolyn raised my bed. Leaning over she fit the valve and deflated the cuff. *I'm afraid no sound will come out.* "Okay Kate, try making a sound," she instructed.

I want to shout. I'm trying to sound out something. I'm trying. I'm trying – "I – I," could be heard faintly. Carolyn listened intently. *Why can't I get any words out? I thought this was supposed to help me speak?*

"Beautiful, now try to take it slowly," Carolyn instructed me. Garbled sounds were produced and with the force of me trying to make a sound, the tiny valve catapulted across the room. *Oops! Watch out!*

"Look out!" Steven shouted ducking his head. Both of them stood back in amazement.

"Well at least we know she has a good set of lungs," Carolyn said laughing. *What happened? I don't understand this!*

"We need to work on this but it will help her a lot," she said. The valve was removed and my cuff on the trachea inflated. "I was told Kate might have aphasia," Steven said. "What is that?"

"Aphasia is a total or partial loss of the ability to use words." She replied, "It appears she understands everything being said to her when I ask simple questions. It will take practice working with the valve," she concluded.

"Are you going to leave the valve with us?" Steven asked. "No, I need to be present when she tries this," Carolyn said putting it in a jar. She then left the room. "Well that was interesting. I can't wait until you can speak again," Steven said. *Neither can I.*

"Let's do some leg exercises," he said pulling the sheets back. *I'm tired from trying to speak. Please let me rest.* Steven moved my legs. "Okay now try to move them back," he said.

I reluctantly did the exercise once, but refused to try anymore. "Good job Kate, one more time," he said. *I'm worn out. I need rest.* "Now you get some rest. I'm going to go out and make sure the nurses chart this," he said. I closed my eyes and dozed off.

While I continued my constant battle to stay alive, Steven fought his constant battle with the insurance company to keep me from being sent to a long term care facility, where I would spend the rest of my life as a water lily. I would get plenty of fresh air and light, but no therapy to help me to walk or talk again. This was a constant, frightening reality for Steven.

He would have lost the fight if my medical condition were more stable. That is why he was always pushing me to change, get better, anything, and documenting every little thing. I cannot imagine how people without strong advocates can possibly make it through the process. Without someone at your side, your chances to survive a serious illness like this are fearfully low.

The best I could do at this point was to sit up with help for thirty minutes each day.

My doctor had ordered me to sit in a cardiac chair three times a day. The following day, Betsy and Ron wheeled this hideous looking chair into my room. *I'm going to sit in that?* "This is a cardiac chair Kate, and we'll sit you up for thirty minutes," Betsy explained. *A cardiac chair? It looks like an execution chair on death row. I don't want to sit in that thing!*

The chair was brought close to the bed, the back lowered. Now it looked like a gurney. Ron slid my body onto it gently, as if I was in a coma. *I hope they know what they are doing.* He then raised the back of the chair until I was sitting upright. *I hate this. I already feel dizzy.* Betsy started placing pillows behind my neck and back for support. Looking back, I now appreciate the expertise in positioning and how Betsy and Ron used pillows, towels, and blankets to make me comfortable. My body ached and my head hurt. It was amazingly painful and exhausting sitting in the chair even for a few minutes.

"Let's wheel Kate near the edge of the door so she can watch what's going on," Betsy said. Ron maneuvered the chair, setting the brakes and making sure the lines would reach the chair from the bed. "I'll be back soon Kate," Betsy said, as she gave me a final check.

I don't want to be left alone! With blurred vision, I couldn't make out the people. I saw the fuzzy, ghostly white shapes of nurses scurrying from room to room. I sat there wondering when the thirty minutes would be up. I wanted to watch Oprah on TV, but the picture was too hazy. *This is hopeless. I cannot stand the pain another second. How can I make it for thirty minutes? Don't these people know I'm sick? Why can't I speak? I'm trapped in my body! I hate this chair. Oh please, I just want to lie down.*

A nurse cheerfully reminded me that I had another ten minutes of sitting in the chair – and wasn't it wonderful to be sitting up again? *I hate this. Anyway, why complain when there is no one here to offer sympathy?*

I closed my eyes to rest. All I was thinking about were my children, wondering what they would be feeling now. I could not remember how long it had been since I had seen them. I knew it was a foolish vanity, but it was also an instinct to protect them. I simply did not want them to see me like this. In fact, I still did not know for sure if I would live, let alone recover; and I did not want my children to remember me the way I looked in ICU.

From the Other Side of the Bed

It's important to set goals for loved ones who cannot set them for themselves. It is also important to set supporting goals for yourself.

My ultimate goal was Kate's full recovery. To accomplish that, she needed a lot of attention and therapy. Putting aside how you may feel about what has happened to medical care in America in the past ten years, it always has been, and still is, very difficult to get insurance companies to spend money. It can be done, it's just not easy.

To get the money spent you have to meet certain criteria; the problem is, you do not intuitively know what standards the insurance company is using when they evaluate your loved one for the purpose of authorizing treatment.

That's where the case manager comes in. The case manager is the liaison between the hospital and the insurance company. The case manager works for the hospital, but sometimes you find you have a case manager who works more for the insurance company than for the hospital.

In all fairness, being a case manager is not an easy job. The case manager's actual employer is the hospital – they are writing the case manager's paychecks – so the case manager's primary concern is supposed to be to make sure the hospital is going to get paid for services given to the patient.

In addition, however, people don't typically go into any branch of the health care professions without an inherent concern and commitment to patients, so please don't think I am saying that the case manager does not care about your loved one. It's just that they have what is almost a conflict of interest woven into their job and it never hurts to remind them that why they became a case manager in the first place was their concern for patients who need treatment.

It is important that you meet the case manager and make her or him your friend and ally. And you need to help them, help you. In doing that, you need to know from the case manager what goals and standards your loved one will have to satisfy in order to get treatment. Case managers can and will tell you if you ask. They usually will not volunteer that information unless you do ask. Most caregivers don't even know that these standards exist let alone what they are. Believe me, if you are going to get the best possible treatment for your loved one, you need to know these things.

Once you know what the insurance companies are looking for, it's up to you to see that they get what they need. The nursing staff is busy taking care of your loved one; their job does not normally include fighting for authorization of treatment.

Make a list of what your loved one needs to do to get treatment, and then make sure that you do everything to see to it that it is not only accomplished, but that it is documented in the patient's medical records.

I admit that I was often a pain in the neck because I was constantly asking (or I should say "telling") the nurses to chart this or that. "Did you see Kate move her toe?" I would say. "Look, come on Kate, THERE! See it? See it? Good! Please put it in her chart."

Of course I told the nurses why I was being so insistent, and since they all wanted the best for Kate, they were willing to cut me some slack. They usually did what I asked with a smile (sometimes a forced smile, but I'll take what I can get).

Always remember that you have to keep at it. I admit now that I cheated – a little. Sometimes, I would save up something so that I could show a little progress or some new thing each week if not every day.

Each week you should meet with the case worker and find out what the goals are. It is a game – a deadly serious game – and the prize is pretty significant. Winning this game can mean the difference between your loved one walking, or never walking again.

Stephanie, my oldest child was scared. "Where's Mom gone?" she would ask Steven every day. "Why can't Mom pick up the phone and talk to me? Don't they have phones in hospitals? Am I going to see her again? I want to see my mom."

Steven kept reassuring her, "She'll be home soon." Yet with each passing day he realized that I was going to be in for the long haul. I had been in the hospital for a couple of weeks. Each day, Steven asked me if Stephanie could come in. *See me? Are you crazy? I don't want her to see me like this.* I longingly gazed at the picture of Stephanie and Rachel on the shelf. *I wish I could be home with my girls. I miss them so much.* Everyday Steven would ask, "Can Stephanie come in today?" Every day I would blink out "No" on the alphabet board. *I don't want my little girl to see me so sick.*

He pleaded with me, "Kate, she wants to see you. She thinks you are dead." He had to convince Stephanie that I hadn't died. *Oh, my poor baby! Stephanie thinks I am dead. I'm not so sure seeing me like this will convince her otherwise. Perhaps they are right, it would be better for everyone if I were dead. God, please help me. What do I do?*

Steven felt he had to have Stephanie see me or she would be scarred for life with a fear of abandonment. He came in one day with my friend Cherri and took a few photos of me with a Polaroid camera. I could have killed him!

"Kate, I'm going to take your photo this morning." *Photo? What the heck is he thinking?* Steven started taking pictures. "I have to show Stephanie you are still alive." I did not want photos taken of me like that. I struggled to turn my head. *I can't escape this. Oh God, please make him stop.* He took five or six images from different angles. *Stop that! I don't want my photo taken. Go away!*

"Try to smile," he said. *Try to smile?* "The girls will be happy to see you haven't died." *Haven't died? Do I look alive to you?*

"Stephanie needs to see you Kate. Can she come to see you?" he pleaded.

Firmly, I kept blinking out, "No." *When is he going to quit asking? No! No! No!*

"Kate, you have to let her see you, she loves you," he pleaded.

I gave up and gave in. *Okay, okay, I'll see her!* I reluctantly blinked out "Yes."

"Can I bring her today?" he asked enthusiastically. "No!" I blinked. *I am not ready to see her today.*

He asked a girlfriend of mine to be at the house when he showed the photos to the girls. "I don't want to be alone Valerie," he said anxiously.

"No problem, I'll help you," she said. He prepared the girls for what they were about to see.

"Girls, sit down next to Daddy. I'm going to let you see a photograph of Mom. She's very sick, but slowly getting better." He pulled one of the prints from his wallet. "This is what your mother looks like in the hospital," he said, handing it to them.

Rachel refused to look at the photograph. She was already referring to the nanny as her mom. Stephanie held the snapshot and paused for a long time while she studied it. "Daddy, what is that?" she asked pointing.

"Oh that's a tube to help Mom breathe, and that funny thing on her arm takes her blood pressure," he said.

"That helps the doctors and nurses make your mother get better," Valerie said.

"How can that help?" she asked puzzled.

"It tells them what is going on inside her body," she explained.

"Oh," Stephanie said gazing at the photo, teardrops starting to run down her cheeks. "This doesn't look like Mom," she said.

Choking back tears, Steven said, "I know Honey, she's very ill."

Suddenly, Stephanie ran out of the room screaming, "No! My mom doesn't look like this!"

Steven turned to Valerie, "This was a mistake. It's too soon to have shown them this."

From the Other Side of the Bed

Our oldest daughter, Stephanie, could not understand what had happened. In her mind, her mother had deserted her. She kept asking me when she could talk to her mother. I told Stephanie that her mother could not talk. She did not believe me. She was convinced that everyone could talk and that there was no such place that does not have a phone.

I knew I had to do something. My child had to know her mother had not deserted her. She needed to know her mother was alive. I wanted to bring Stephanie to the hospital, but that was impossible for the moment. Kate was adamant that she did not want the children to see her in her condition. I could not put any more pressure on Kate, so I was powerless to bring mother and child together.

The next best thing was to show Stephanie a photo of her mom. It is a horrible photo, sad and full of pain. I wasn't sure I should show it to my daughter. I walked around with it in my wallet for a few days before I showed it to her. Her reaction was one of grief and denial. I shouldn't have done it, yet I knew that Stephanie had to see her mom and soon. In a three-year-old's mind a nanny can become Mom awfully fast. Resentment, confusion and sense of abandonment can occur that may never be undone.

Stephanie had hidden the photo. "That's not my mother. I know she wants to see me. Let me visit her Daddy," she pleaded tugging at his shirt. She didn't believe I was that ill. "I want to see my mom," she cried.

He sat her on his lap. "I know Honey, you will," he said gently rocking her in his arms. "We need to pray that Mom keeps getting better." One afternoon, he asked me again about Stephanie coming in to see me. I gave up. *This guy just doesn't let up! Fine! I don't care anymore.* I reluctantly blinked "Yes."

Overjoyed, he hurried out of the room to call the nanny. "Amanda, bring Stephanie down. Kate's ready to see her," he instructed. "Hurry before Kate changes her mind," he hastily added.

I was doing leg exercises with my therapist, Betsy, when Rhonda appeared at the door knocking gently, "Stephanie is here, Kate." *She's here already? I'm working with Betsy. I'm not ready for this.* My husband came into view holding Stephanie.

Betsy pulled the sheets up on the bed. "Hi Stephanie, come on in and see your mom," she said. "We were doing some exercises."

Stephanie clung to her dad, her arms tight around his neck. "Go over and see Mom," he said, putting her down.

Stephanie, it's Mum. I wish I could reach out and hug you. Don't be scared Honey. I miss you so much; I just want to hold you. She stood there staring at me. The surroundings frightened her. I lay there looking at her, yearning to touch her. *What are you thinking? You look frightened. If only I could hold your hand.* Stephanie didn't quite know how to react. She hesitated taking a step forward. *That's it Honey, come over to Mum.*

She was afraid, and ran back to her father, "Daddy, Daddy."

He bent down, scooping her up in his arms. "It's okay Honey, that's your mom."

She didn't respond except to turn her head away from me and start crying, letting out the most awful wail. I shall never forget the sound of her anguished cry. Steven said he could have sworn that both Stephanie and I were screaming in unison. "Take me home Daddy," she said in between sobs. *I wish you had not brought her in. This has been too much for both of us!*

Betsy tried to encourage everyone by making light conversation. "Stephanie, Mom's getting better, she'll be home soon," she said. The tension in the air was so thick you could cut it with a knife. I lay there with my eyes watering. *I just want to hold my little girl.* It was traumatic for both of us. Even Betsy fought back tears.

"I think I had better take her home," Steven said. "I'll be back later tonight Kate."

After they left, Betsy positioned me in the bed. She rolled some towels and placed them at my feet to prevent foot drop. "Oh Kate, your daughter is darling," she said. *Yes. I wish I could be with her. I miss them both.* Betsy left the room so I could rest. *This is the hardest time in my life. Why God, why do I have to endure this? Why do my babies have to endure this?*

Ten tips that psychologist, Judith Carl, Ph.D., has found to help children through the process of Mom and Dad having any type of adversity.

1.   Expect that your children (of all ages) will have feelings, thoughts and opinions about whatever the issue/problem is.

2.   Even though you may not talk about the problem in earshot of your children, they will pick up the vibes that there is something wrong.

3.   It helps to calm children, to let them know that there is a problem. What you tell them of the details depends on the issue, crisis, or problem.

4.   Certain crises need to be talked about in as much detail as children want; i.e., accidents, terrorism, life-threatening events, hospitalizations. They need to be reassured that the other parent will be there to talk about it as they have a need to. Some children need to hear and be told that it is not their fault.

5.   If it is a life situation; i.e. possible divorce, separation, etc., children need to know there is a problem, that they did not cause it, and that they are loved by both parents. However, they do NOT need to hear and know the details of the problem.

6.   Keep children out of the middle of the problem. For example, do not have them be the messenger between the parents, or ask them to choose which parent they want to live with, or ask how they feel about what Mom or Dad did or said.

7.   Acknowledge your children's feelings. Examples: "I can see you're upset about this … You must really be worried about … I am here and available to talk to you whenever you have a question or just want to talk. Let me know."

8.   It is okay to let them see your emotions. It helps them to see that you have feelings too. Feelings are different from details. Feelings are sadness, hurt, fear, relief, joy, calmness, anticipation, etc., that surround the details of the situation.

Showing your feelings lets them know that it is okay for them to have their own feelings.

9.   Consider some outside counseling or therapy for your children if it seems that they are having difficulties because of the situation or crisis. You may see it in their school grades, detachment, if they are normally outgoing, isolation, a sudden change in their behavior at home or school; i.e. acting out, extreme introversion, reduced eating, or binge eating, problems with friends, etc.

10.   Asking for help for yourself and/or family demonstrates strength and courage. You and your family, including your children, deserve to have the support, guidance, and help in getting through any crisis or life situation.

Chapter Five

~

The Light

The only family I had nearby was my husband and the girls. My biological family was in New Zealand. The first night I was in the hospital, Steven called them and left a message on their voicemail to call him as soon as possible. Briefly, he explained that I was in the hospital with a suspected stroke.

Mum's first reaction was, "That's not possible. Kate's too healthy." She phoned my father at work, and he too was stunned, as were my siblings. My brother Tony, a pharmacist, thought it was probably a severe migraine, "She's too fit to have had a stroke." Steven kept my parents informed and after numerous calls between the States and New Zealand, my parents realized how serious things were.

From the Other Side of the Bed

There is an old saying that no man is poor who has friends. The best investment in time I ever made in my life was to get involved in my community. A few months before Kate's stroke, I received a license to be a pastor. I had thought about the possibility of moving to New Zealand to start a church.

63

The night before Kate had her stroke was my first night, and as it turned out, my last as a pastor. I thought I was going to be involved in helping people, but it turned out I was going to be the one getting the help.

I cannot stress enough how our church helped us. They took the pressure of every day life off my shoulders. I did not have to worry about who would watch the kids, or about feeding myself or my children. Twenty-four hours a day, seven days a week, there was someone at my house or at the hospital to help me. I knew they would be there for us, indefinitely if need be.

The women took turns making meals and watching the children. My wife had been very active in the church and every woman in her Bible study group pitched in to share our burden.

I got up every morning spent a few moments with my children and then it was off to the hospital. When I got to the hospital, there was always someone from the church there. I remember one woman, Sharon, whose job was to force me to eat something healthy every day. She had a tough time of it. I lost about 25 pounds while Kate was in the hospital.

Kate was never alone. When I had to go home, someone filled in for me and sat with Kate. These people (I call them angels) visited Kate in two to three hour shifts. God bless the 3 a.m. to 5 a.m. shift. God bless them all.

Day after day, the waiting room in ICU was filled with people. A member donated a journal for everyone to sign and express their prayers and good wishes for me. Women from the church sat quietly by my bedside reading the Bible and praying. It was a one-way conversation. All I could do was listen.

I wonder if they know I understand what's being said. Nurses came in and out continuing with their daily duties. *Why God? Why me? Why am I hooked up to machines and totally helpless?* Women constantly massaged lotion on my feet, and others gave me manicures. Rolled up wash cloths were placed in the palms of my tightly clenched fists, or my fingernails would dig into my palms and cut the skin.

Today, I still keep my nails trimmed to prevent them from doing the same thing when I sleep. Even as I write this my paralyzed left hand is clenched tight in a fist. When this happens, which it does constantly, I have to gently open each finger to get my hand to relax. Acrylic nails are definitely out of the question!

Often friends would wash my hair. My hair was long, requiring a whole can of dry shampoo. *This hurts to have my hair washed with this stuff.* After the shampoo process, my hair was braided. *At least my friends care enough to take care of the little details.* I was always relieved when it was over. *Am I ever going to make it out of here? Please, God let me have my life back.*

One evening my friends, Theresa and Lisa, were in my room visiting. *It feels good having my feet massaged, but I have this annoying strand of hair by my eye. How can I tell them how annoying it is?* I was so frustrated. *I just want to scratch my face!* They noticed I was trying to tell them something.

"Do you need a nurse?" Theresa asked. *No, I need this hair off my face!*

"Are you comfortable?" Lisa asked. *No. It's this strand of hair that's bugging me.*

"I wonder what she's trying to tell us." Theresa mused, a puzzled look on her face. *No, I am certainly not comfortable; I just want this removed. Are we playing Jeopardy? This is a simple thing, yet it's so hard for me to communicate. I've taken so much for granted.*

The women tried to guess what I needed. It was like playing charades without being able to use your body. *It's no use! I'll never be able to tell you. Is this how my life is going to be?*

After a lengthy amount of time, they finally guessed what was bothering me. "I know; it's a hair that's bugging you." Lisa said excitedly running her hand across my face. *Yes! Yes! Finally you guessed.*

"Kate, I'm sorry that took us so long to figure that out," Theresa said. *I can't believe how frustrating that was!*

I was desperately sick for the seventy days I was in ICU. I was listed as "critical" for sixty-nine of those days. I had lived through the trauma of an assault to my brain, but at a dreadful price. I weighed only ninety-eight pounds. The doctors knew I would be faced with serious medical complications. The first complication was mild, or would have been for a normal person. It was a small blood clot in my leg. The doctor caught it early before it could lead to another stroke. Technically this was phlebitis. In my condition, if the clot had traveled to my lungs, I would have died.

One day Steven saw one of my fingers move ever so slightly. It took him two days to get anyone to believe him. Suddenly, here was this man telling the doctors that this totally paralyzed woman had moved her finger. The doctor thought he was crazy and politely told him that family members often see what they want to see. Steven was not about to have his wife's efforts ignored. Steven would not back off.

He made me move my finger several times to be certain I could do it on command and then he tracked down the doctor and insisted that he come see for himself. I almost lost my chance to qualify for therapy at this point because I had exhausted myself repeating this simple task. When the doctor did come, I could not move a thing. I lost all power to move from sheer exhaustion.

Steven knew the doctor would not come back in to see me move. He went to convince the nurses. Finally, I was able to move a finger slightly for a nurse and Steven made sure she noted it in the chart for the doctor to see. The doctor felt duty bound to check out the chart notes, and later when he was in my room, he thought maybe he saw me move. He simply couldn't believe his own eyes, if it was movement, could it be voluntary. Before he believed I had voluntarily moved any part of my body, he insisted on coming back to see it two more times.

After the third time, he told Steven that he wasn't easily impressed, but this was extraordinary and he thought there was a possibility that I could achieve a significant recovery.

From the Other Side of the Bed

$\mathcal{A}$s a lawyer you must remember that the guy in the black robe always has the last word. In the medical world, the guy in the black robe is the doctor. He wears white instead of black, but he still has enormous power.

I had to deal with Kate's doctor in such a way that we could both help Kate. It was difficult at first because of the conflict we had early on when I wanted Kate treated with heparin.

I knew that I was going to have to push this man but not so far that he went out the door. I hate to say this, but I think it helps if the medical staff knows that someone is looking over their shoulders. I had made it very clear that if the doctors missed anything, they were going to get sued; and that I was watching and documenting every-thing. So now I had to do a little fence mending – not always my strong suit.

When I began talking to the medical staff about Kate's progress, no one believed me. They did believe that it would not be wise to ignore me. It is true, the squeaky wheel gets the grease.

Of course, I knew that there were plenty more doctors in Los Angeles. If the doctors were not going to go along with me, I would have fired them. I wanted to avoid that kind of conflict. I was also totally determined to be listened to. There simply was too much at stake.

When I finally got the doctor to admit he could trust his own eyes, I was relieved, but not surprised. Now we had a ball game.

Officially, I was still scheduled to be put into a skilled nursing facility – to simply be planted on a porch like a potted plant and left to soak up sunshine. The odds of making any significant recovery were less than one in a million. No one believed I had any real potential for recovery except Steven and my fellow church members. They all believed I would be granted a miracle.

Making things worse, Steven told the doctors that while praying at my bedside, he had seen the room turn bright as the sun, and felt the presence of God. From that point on, he told everyone I would have a miracle. I know he believes he saw the light and believed I would get better. It seems that Steven was right on both counts, certainly he was proven correct. I was going to get better.

From the Other Side of the Bed

Why do so many Christians say they believe the Bible, but are shocked when something in it – like healing – actually takes place? I never quite understood that.

As mentioned earlier, Steven had kept close contact with my parents and, at the request of my doctors, had called them to learn my family history. When he told them that I had either a stroke or a brain tumor, my mother responded, "Strokes do not run in our family, however, Kate had an uncle who died of a brain tumor at the age of 46, maybe that's what it is."

My mother called my aunt to get more details. My aunt phoned Steven back with the information while Mum waited anxiously for further news. When Steven did call my parents with the new information that it was in fact a stroke, both clung to each other weeping with relief.

I had survived the stroke and now the doctors found that I was growing pseudomonas bacterium in my trachea tube. That would not have been so frightening except the tested culture showed that it was not responsive to any known antibiotic. This was a super bug that only grew in hospitals and if it spread into my lungs, I would die. The doctors felt helpless. They could not find any antibiotic to treat it. We were fortunate that the man running the lab at the hospital was a member of our church. Usual protocol for a culture was every two days. Dr. Kolodney and the lab conspired to do a culture for me every two hours.

This was one of Steven's lowest moments. He waited for each successive culture to come back from the lab. The tests showed that the bacterium was growing faster and faster. It seemed that having lived through the stroke, I would die of a glorified sore throat.

The doctors told Steven I only had two or three days to live unless a solution could be found. That was the wrong thing to tell Steven! He started to hound the doctors working my case. "What if we do this? What if we do that? Can we try this? How about that?" Steven questioned Dr. Kolodney mercilessly.

Dr. Kolodney spent a whole hour talking with Steven, and they finally decided to call in an infectious disease specialist. He came, took one look at me and explained to Steven and the doctor that he might have some magic. He sprayed what seemed like Lysol into the tube, and the bacterium was killed dead on the spot, just like in the Raid commercial.

From the Other Side of the Bed

Y ou cannot be passive when you are the advocate for your loved one. You have to remember that the doctor has lots of patients but you have only one ill son, daughter or spouse.

In addition, medicine has become so complicated that no one doctor can have all the answers. Lung doctors tend to think only in terms of lungs. Neurologists may not notice or recognize an infection. It's up to you to get your doctors to talk to each other. Try to be diplomatic of course, but don't hesitate to get tough and demanding if you must. This isn't easy for those of you who have been conditioned to "respect authority" but you simply cannot count on the doctors talking to each other on their own.

Also keep in mind that the doctors saw Kate 20 minutes a day; I was with her 20 hours a day. The nurse and you know the most about what is going on. Always make friends with the nurse. Ask questions and then ask more questions.

Dr Kolodney saved Kate's life but he did not think of calling in an infectious disease specialist. I did. It's not that the doctor didn't care, he did care; and when I asked him to speak with me, he took the time to answer a dozen questions, which finally led to an answer that saved Kate's life.

The point is that you cannot assume that even very caring doctors will think of everything or take care of the problem on their own. You cannot even assume the doctors know about the problem. You have to stay on top of what is going on and sometimes force the medical staff to deal with your issues. Without you, your loved one's chances for survival may be significantly reduced.

The doctors had been trying to treat me by giving antibiotics through my IVs. The medicine could not reach the point where it would have been a strong enough dose to kill the infection in the trachea tube. By spraying it directly on the site of the infection, a large enough dose could be delivered to kill the bacteria. Steven sat hour after hour as the bacteria count continued to go down, and then out. I had now survived my third medical crisis.

My fourth crisis was not life threatening, but was certainly one of the most hellish things that I had to endure. Since I could not receive nourishment through an IV tube, a G-tube had been placed in my stomach. Through the tube I received Ensure and other food supplements. Perhaps, because of the antibiotic or just because of my immobility, I was now unable to have a bowel movement. Ensure through a tube is far from tasty, but it does keep you free from feeling hungry. I was so constipated that the doctors were forced to turn off the feeding tube. Then the count started: Day one, no food and no bowel movement. Day two, the same. Day three, still neither food nor a bowel movement.

I had now been without food for 72 hours. I was starving. This continued for another five days. As the days passed, I thought I would go insane. The hunger pains were unbearable. I was screaming in my mind, "Don't you know I need to eat?" I could think of nothing but eating and having a bowel movement! The pressure on my stomach was awful. Up to this point the bagful of Ensure passing through the tube, sounded pretty good. *I just want something! Feed me. Don't let me die. For God's sake, somebody feed me!*

Day eight, still nothing happened. Finally on day nine, I had a bowel movement and the doctors were able to gradually start me back on Ensure. The agony of going without food was a constant pain that lasted not hours like the surgery to put the tube in, but days. My whole body cried out for food. It would take another week to get me up to a dose that would allow me to be free from hunger pains.

From the Other Side of the Bed

I never felt more helpless than during this intermission in hell. It was unimaginable. The pain was evident in Kate's eyes after her stroke, you could not miss it and you could not ignore it.

My first concern for Kate had been to make sure that she got sufficient pain medication, but I was unsuccessful because Kate was not allowed pain medication because of certain complications that it would create. That was a reality that had to be accepted.

Now her expression had worsened, if that was possible. You could tell when you were in her room that you were in the presence of pure, unrelenting agony.

The minutes burned slowly away second after second, no food, no relief from the unending pain.

There Kate lies alone in silence in the dark with God. Whatever her thoughts were, she could share them with no one. I looked on as the fast continued and began to wonder how anyone could continue to live in the face of such horror. I would have given up long before now if it had been me in that hospital bed.

In her condition, Kate really could not understand what was going on. She had no way of knowing when or if she would ever get better.

It was enough to make me despair – but I could not. It was my job to make each second just a little easier. The doctors supplied medical treatment; I supplied hope.

I filled every long painful second with music and companionship. Worship music played 24 hours a day, people offered encouragement and prayer 24 hours a day. Still, I cannot, as I look back, even begin to understand how it was that Kate made the decision moment after moment, day after day, to take her next breath.

After that ordeal, I was hauled out of my room and put on a sling like a cow or pig and moved onto a scale. This continued once a week, very early in the mornings. *What is happening?* I felt the cold air as the sheets were gathered back. *Please let me sleep. Give me my covers back!* I was in a dreamlike state. I remember being moved around while I kept my eyelids closed. I was rolled onto my side, while one nurse slipped a heavy piece of canvas under me. They repeated the process on my other side. I heard the sharp clicking of metal and the cranking of a handle. *What are they doing?* Without warning, I felt myself gradually lifting and being suspended in the air. My eyelids quickly opened. *What's happening?*

"Just relax Kate, we are weighing you," said one of the nurses. *Weighing me?* The noise of the cranking stopped and I remained there while the nurses wrote in my chart. I feel tremendous empathy now when I see a helpless animal being lifted in the air from a dangerous situation. Suspended in the air, one is powerless. That's how I felt. What seemed like an eternity actually took only a few minutes. *Isn't there a more dignified way of weighing someone?* The nurses would lower the device and put me back in bed and pull up the sheets. *How am I supposed to go back to sleep?*

This machine, designed for weighing paralyzed patients, is called a "sling scale." Since my stroke, the hospital has acquired a device that's attached to the bed which weighs the patient. My weight over the six weeks in ICU went down considerably. My once-toned body faded to a mere 90 pounds. Talk about your 90 pound weakling, I had nowhere to go, but up.

The pain and loneliness were so overwhelming that I could hardly tell what was reality and what was a dream. Hours had no meaning. Days had no meaning. It was all one endless eternal dark and painful journey through hell.

Steven continuously phoned my parents, asking them to come. Mum and Dad felt a trip later on would be better. Dad was self-employed, and could not leave his business. It was their livelihood.

From the Other Side of the Bed

I now found myself in open conflict with my in-laws. They just could not comprehend what was going on and did not realize that things over time would only get worse. Kate's parents wanted me to stop my foolishness and quit living at the hospital. In their mind, my place was at work. They felt that Kate was a strong-willed woman who had no need for me to be bothering her with my constant attention. Of course, that was anything but true. Kate needed me there and if anything she needed more, not less attention.

I am not sure what value you put on life. Many people, when faced with the loss of a loved one, would gladly write a blank check if they could. How many rich people have prayed that old man cancer would take American Express?

I would pay an awful price for not going back to work.
In the end we would lose millions of dollars, but we did not
lose Kate.

While at the hospital one morning Steven approached the charge nurse. "Could you do me a favor?" he asked. "Kate's mother does not realize how sick Kate is. She thinks I'm exaggerating. If I call her will you talk to her?"

"Sure, I'll talk with her," the nurse said. He dialed the number. A brief conversation took place.

"My daughter isn't going to die, is she?" Mum asked.

"I can't honestly say," the nurse replied. "She is in critical condition, Mrs. Adamson, and has been for a long time. Kate is very sick and I know if she was my daughter, I'd want to be here with her."

There was a brief silence. Mum answered quietly, "Thank you nurse. I'll come straight away." The New Zealand Airline plane landed in Los Angeles on a Sunday. Mum was anxious to see me but had to go through the long customs line before finally seeing Steven. The two had only met twice in person. Mum explained to him, "I would like to go straight to the hospital to see Kate."

In the car, Steven showed her a couple of photos he had taken of me in ICU.

"Surely she doesn't look like this!" Mum commented.

"I'm afraid so," Steven replied. She sat in the back saying nothing. Despite the 15 hour flight and her exhaustion, she was overwhelmed and anxious to see me that afternoon. Steven noticed that she appeared to have caught a cold. He suggested she wear a surgical mask and gloves when she came near me.

They arrived at Torrance Memorial Hospital mid-afternoon. It was a beautiful day for the outside world, but Mum paid no attention to the surroundings. All she wanted to do was see her daughter. They made their way to ICU.

My friend Penny came into my room. "Your mom is here. Just enjoy her and let her love you," she said. *Mum is here?*

Moments later I saw her standing in the doorway, her face strained with worry. She paused for a moment glancing around the room at the faces of the women standing by my bed. A couple of women from church were rubbing lotion on my hands and feet. I looked at Mum and opened my mouth to cry out, but no sound came. *Mum, Mum, you are here. Thank God you have come!*

As happy as I was to see her standing at the foot of my bed, it also scared me. I knew I must be very sick for her to have come that far. Total paralysis, feeding tubes, starvation, and the attention of all of Christendom wasn't enough of a clue – it was seeing Mum standing there that gave me the incredible realization that I might actually die. *Where's Dad? Why isn't he here?* I could see the tears filling her eyes. My mother never cried. *Mum, I wish I could speak to you. I have so much to tell you.*

Jenny, another friend, was massaging my arms, "See Katie, your mom did come. Do you have a cold?" Jenny asked my mother.

"A slight one. I just left winter in New Zealand," Mum replied in her thick accent.

"We need you to put a mask on if you want to come close," Jenny explained.

Ignoring protocol, Mum said brusquely, "I'm her mother, and nothing I do could possibly hurt her." Teardrops trickled down her cheeks as she approached my bed. Pulling a handkerchief from her pocket she quickly wiped her tears and leaned over gently kissing me on the forehead. "Why Katie, why?" Mum asked, weeping. "You remind me of that little girl when you used to get sick," she said stroking my forehead and smiling. Hiding her emotions, she prattled on about her plans.

She would be here five weeks. Mum chit-chatted about everyone else in New Zealand and told me there would be a surprise when she had to leave. *I wonder what that is. Must be a family member coming over. I don't care about a surprise. I just want to be normal and go home.* I previously had plans with my brother Tony to visit Disneyland in August, but not anymore.

"Your sister and brother are planning to come in August to spend some time with you," Mum cheerfully said. *No, I don't want them to see me like this.* "Your father couldn't come. He had to stay home and take care of the business. He sends his love and I'm to call him every day to keep him informed. Everyone sends love." As she chatted on and on, I relaxed into sleep with the feeling that Mum was there and I would be okay. I remember fading off with the realization that my stroke happened on her birthday. *This is one birthday she won't forget.*

A nurse came in asking everyone to leave while she attended to my needs. Mum left with the ladies and sat outside. She had brought some photos of my siblings and me. Like a proud mother she showed everyone her family. As everyone came back into the room, Steven explained that he was driving Mum home so she could get some rest and see the girls. "I'm very tired Katie babes; it was a long flight," she said. *Take me with you, Mum – don't leave me.* Mum kissed me on the cheek and left the room.

From the Other Side of the Bed

I *thought that when Kate's mother showed up, things would become easier for me. I was living an awful pace – getting up early and going to bed late. The average night would see me home well after 1 a.m. I would not leave for the night until I was sure that Kate was asleep.*

I got up in the morning had a quick breakfast with my children. Every morning, the kids attached themselves to my legs like Velcro, screaming, "Daddy don't go, don't go. Stay! Daddy!" I had to have the babysitter pull them off me and it broke my heart every single time.

I arrived at the hospital in time to talk to the doctors during rounds. I stayed until the evening. Then I went home for a short dinner and then back to the hospital. Once again each night I had to have the girls pried off my legs. I tried to explain to the children that their mom's life depended on my being with her, but how do you explain that to a three year old and an eighteen month old?

Chapter Six

~

Paralyzed but not Powerless

*I*t was a comfort knowing Mum was here. I knew she would keep things in order around the house. Mum enjoyed meeting Betsy and watching her therapy routine.

The nurses enjoyed her New Zealand accent. "Does your daughter sound like you?" they would ask. It seemed odd, that many people had taken care of me for weeks, yet they did not know the sound of my voice.

On Monday morning, while watching my therapy session, Mum asked Betsy if it would be possible to hold me in her arms. *Oh Mum, not now! They are too busy for that. Besides I don't want to be embarrassed!*

"I just want to hold my baby," she said politely. Her voice sounded muffled through the mask that she finally gave in to wearing.

"Oh sure," Betsy said. *Oh no, don't you people realize how much effort that's going to take?* Carefully Ron and Betsy sat me on the edge of the bed, being cautious not to pull any lines.

"Oh, thank you," Mum said, coming over to me. She wrapped her arms tight around me. My frail body felt her warmth. *Mum, I can smell your perfume as you are holding me. I love you. I know this is hard on you too. I'm 33 years old, but right now, I'm your baby again.*

79

As she gently held me, I could hear her quietly weeping. *What's going to happen to me Mum?* "Oh Katie, I love you darling. It breaks my heart to see you like this," she whispered. She glanced up at Betsy. "Kate is awfully thin. There is nothing left of her but skin and bones. Isn't there something the doctor can do?" *Just like a mum!*

"You can speak to Dr. Kolodney about building her up more," said Betsy. *Mum! You always felt I was too thin.* The very next day I was increased to 1,000 calories a day through my feeding tube. Mum was on the job. I felt sorry for the doctors, with her and Steven, they didn't have a chance.

Mum watched Betsy stretching the heel cord on the back of my ankle. The stretch felt good. The procedure made her curious. "What does that do?" she asked.

Betsy paused for a moment. "This is to prevent her foot from developing foot drop. In fact, Mrs. Adamson, it would be beneficial if Kate wore some high-top tennis shoes a few hours everyday." *Tennis shoes? Tennis shoes in bed. No way!*

Mum was only too willing to help, "What size do I get?"

Betsy replied, "You will want a couple of sizes bigger than she normally wears. Right now her feet are swollen."

The problem was to have the tennis shoes fit snug enough, but not so tight that they hurt. Mum and my friend, Deborah, made several trips to the local stores trying to find the right pair. It was a guessing game to see if they would fit and not hurt. *I don't want to wear shoes in bed. These are hideous!*

They finally found a pair that won Betsy's approval. I wore the shoes four hours a day, to keep my feet in an upright position. The tops of the socks were cut off, to make them easier to slip onto my feet, which were constantly cold from poor circulation.

I loved seeing Mum visit each day. She delicately smoothed lotion on my face and arms which were dry and scaly from the blood pressure cuff being left on. She knew just where to scratch, and it felt wonderful. She combed and braided my hair. *Someone should probably cut my hair, but I've lost too much to lose anything more.*

Mum chatted about everyone back home trying to take my mind off my troubles. "I've bought you some of your favorite licorice Kate," she said eagerly. "I filled an empty shoe box so you will have plenty." *A shoe box full? I can't even swallow water.*

I was thirsty all the time. I had no swallowing reflexes. I had to settle for mouth swabs or occasionally Mum would sneak me ice chips rubbing them on and around my lips. *A big bottle of Gatorade would be great. I can just taste it.* I've never liked it, and I don't know why, but for some reason I dreamed about Gatorade; its salty sweet flavor pouring down my throat in great refreshing gulps.

Mum constantly rolled the swabs around my lips and inside my mouth. The lemon tasting swabs didn't quench my thirst. My lips were parched and cracked, so she kept rubbing lip balm on them. At mid-morning she briefly left to grab a bite to eat in the cafeteria. *Thank goodness no one eats around me. The smell of food would drive me insane!*

Steven began the long, hard process of getting me accepted into a rehabilitation program. I hate to tell you that the program I finally did get into has since been modified. That program probably restored the quality of life I have today. It is, therefore, even harder than it was in 1995 to get the necessary help. In 1985, the average hospital stay for a stroke like mine would have been about nine months. Now, one is lucky to get six weeks.

To recover, I would need physical therapy and lots of it. The cost would be astronomical. Freeman Hospital was asking $18,000 a week for just the bed. On top of that, medication and doctors' fees would be added.

From the Other Side of the Bed

I wanted Kate to have the best therapy possible. My choices, however, were theoretically limited by what the insurance company was willing to approve. Blue Cross, our insurance company, had a contract with several facilities. A contract means that Blue Cross had a negotiated rate that they had agreed to pay the hospital for providing treatment.

My investigation led me to believe that Kate's best chance was to go to Freeman Hospital, a local hospital with an excellent reputation. The problem was that Freeman Hospital charged $18,000 a week for treatment. That is a lot of money, especially compared to the contract price that Blue Cross was willing to pay, about $800 a week.

Unfortunately, Freeman Hospital did not have a contract with Blue Cross. I got a call from my insurance agent. She wanted me to choose another hospital because Freeman Hospital was not covered on my policy. I told her to say nothing to anyone and that I would pay out of my pocket if I could not convince the insurance company to pick up the cost. Hillary, our agent, was pretty clear I had no chance of getting the insurance company to pick up the bill. She was wrong. I did get them to pay the bill, even though, at the time, the outcome was far from certain.

I wanted Kate to be close enough so I could visit. I wanted her in the best possible program. Choosing Freeman Hospital meant I would be on the hook for about $70,000 a month – for the hospital alone. With a three month stay, that bill, together with the doctor bills, medication, and other treatments, was going to amount to over half a million. I was also losing $30,000 to $50,000 a month by closing my law office.

Well, money is for a rainy day and it sure was raining. I chose Freeman Hospital. I took advantage of a clerk who did not pay proper attention and authorized a transfer there. I figured I would work out the whole thing with the hospital and the insurance company. If I could not work it out, then so be it.

As it was, with a little gentle persuasion, I got Blue Cross to step up to the plate and work something out with *them. The hospital agreed to treat Kate for $800 a week instead of $18,000. I am not sure if I could have done this without being a lawyer. Remember, I am not the only lawyer in the country. If you need help, get a lawyer. It never hurts to let the staff know that someone is looking over their shoulder.*

One day, a lady showed up unannounced by my bed. She began asking Steven all kinds of questions. She had a clipboard and made notes as he responded. I did not realize at the time that my whole future rested with this woman, and with her report, my fate would be determined. She seemed pleasant and talked about my being admitted into their program and what they offered. *What the heck is she talking about? I don't even know this woman.*

Steven made dozens of calls and found that Freeman Hospital had the best program in Los Angeles, the entire country as a matter of fact. He opted for me to be transferred there. He was told I would be accepted. Unbeknownst to him, there was no intention on the part of the hospital to accept me. Steven was told I would be transferred to Freeman Hospital only if I could spend two days on a regular floor to show I was stable enough to be moved. If the insurance companies and hospitals had their way, all I would get out of this was a one-way ticket to a vegetable stand.

Mum had been in the United States for a couple of days when I was finally moved out of ICU onto another floor. *I'm finally leaving ICU. I'm nervous. I'm familiar with the nurses here.* Steven insisted I be put into a private room away from any sick patients. The doctor wanted to transfer me to a medical floor, but Steven wanted me to go to a surgical floor where there would be less chance of contracting an infection. Dr. Kolodney was amazed that Steven had thought the problem out in such depth. He immediately agreed. In ICU each patient was assigned one nurse. On the surgical floor one nurse was supposed to handle seven patients. The reality was one nurse for twelve patients.

From the Other Side of the Bed

*B*efore Kate could be transferred to Rehab, she had to be able to survive without the constant attention she received in ICU, for a full day and night. That meant she would have to be able to manage her secretions so she could get by with no more than three suctionings an hour. That was no easy task for her.

As her caregiver, once again I was able to make a difference. The doctor wanted to have Kate transferred to a medical floor for her one day stay, but I insisted on her being placed on a surgical floor. I did not want her around potentially contagious people. Her chance of getting an infection on a medical floor was far greater than on a surgical floor. A common infection could kill her. I got my way.

Did it make a difference? Of course, we will never know, but it did mean that Kate would have a better chance. Was I smarter than her doctors? No, but I cared more about her personally. I thought about her care more constantly and, therefore, I had something important to say.

If your loved one is in the hospital you may not be smarter than your doctor, but you do care more. Keep thinking, keep asking questions and keep making the doctors answer you.

Mum followed alongside the bed as an attendant wheeled me down the hallway. "This is a good sign Katie babes. It means you are getting better," she said. *I just want to go home Mum.*

I was taken to the sixth floor where I stayed for a couple of days. The room was small and Mum put the photos of my daughters where I could see them. I was not quite ready for a regular room; I was still connected with too many tubes. Compared to ICU, the surgical room was paradise.

Mum was given the opportunity to stay the night in the bed next to me. *There's no way she'll do that. The noise of the machines will drive her crazy.* I was surprised to hear she was planning to stay with me. *Wow! She is going to sleep overnight?*

She came that afternoon with her small overnight bag. It was reassuring to know she was there. Mum made herself comfortable and I drifted off to sleep with her sitting up against the wall reading her book. The bathroom door was slightly open letting enough light in for her to see. Occasionally, I'd open my eyes to see if she was still there. She probably got very little sleep that night but I felt safe having her there.

Steven was able to get a good night's sleep for the first time since my stroke. He had been spending fifteen hours a day with me. Besides that he had to be a father to our daughters.

On his early morning rounds, Dr. Kolodney saw Mum sleeping by me. "Good morning June, you stayed with your daughter last night?" he said.

"Good morning doctor. Yes, I slept in the spare bed. I'm concerned with Kate being on sleeping medication. Can we get her off that doctor?" she asked. *Mum! Are you crazy? I need this. You don't have to try to sleep with a tube hanging out of your throat!*

"Mrs. Adamson, right now is not the appropriate time to take a patient off sleeping medication." *Thank goodness.* "I can assure you she won't get addicted," Dr. Kolodney told her. He asked Mum to step outside for a moment.

In the hallway he put his hand on her arms, "Your daughter will be fine, she'll probably have a limp but she'll be able to live with that." *Damn! I can't hear what he's saying.* I listened intently. I could barely make out what he was saying, but I knew I heard the word limp. *I'm going to have a limp? Limping means walking.* I was excited to think this doctor believed in my chances for recovery.

I spent three long drawn-out days in anticipation of being transferred to rehab. *When can I go to rehab?* Dr. Kolodney came by on his daily rounds. "Hi Kate. How are you this morning?" he asked. *How am I? I want out of here.*

"I think she's trying to ask you something," Steven said, grabbing the alphabet board, and asking me to blink as he pointed to each letter. Dr. Kolodney stood by watching in amazement.

I slowly blinked out, "Will I die?"

"W …" Steven said going along each row, writing the letter down. "I … L …" he said. Then starting at the beginning he went through each row again. "Will I die?" He quickly sounded out.

Yes, that's what I'm trying to ask. I waited patiently for the doctor's response. Dr. Kolodney took my hand, "No, you are not going to die. We are getting you transferred to a rehab hospital and getting you back on your feet – quite literally. Just don't give up."

Steven and Dr. Kolodney walked down the hallway. "We need to get her transferred and make this come true quickly or she might give up her will to live," Dr. Kolodney said. "I've been a doctor for many years and I've never seen anyone go through this kind of ordeal and walk away from it."

"Yes, I saw a light in Kate's eyes when you told her she was going to walk," Steven said.

From the Other Side of the Bed

*W*hen Dr. Kolodney finally saw the light and acknowl-edged what I had believed in all along, that Kate was going to get better, I was tempted to ask, "What part of faith and prayer did you not understand?" But I didn't.

There was some confusion as to whether I was going to Freeman Hospital. The doctor kept waiting for an ambulance. On the third day, Steven paged Dr. Kolodney to find out why it hadn't arrived. "The ambulance will be there at 10 a.m. tomorrow. There was a problem with the paperwork. Don't worry. We'll get her transferred," he said. *Why am I still here? I thought I was being transferred.*

Bright and early the next day, Mum was ready with some things that I would need in my new hospital room. The lobby was full of friends waiting to say goodbye to me. The morning came and went with no sign of an ambulance to transfer me. *What is wrong? How can they make me wait like this?* No ambulance came that day. Suddenly, I was wracked with fear.

Dr. Kolodney asked Steven to step out of the room to have a talk. They both walked back to the doctor's office. Dr. Kolodney retrieved my file on the computer screen which noted that I had been denied admission to Freeman Hospital. "I don't understand what's going on," he said.

"Why would the hospital deny her?" Steven asked.

"I don't know, but if she hasn't been transferred by noon tomorrow, let's meet in the staff lounge and find out what's going on," Dr. Kolodney said.

With a confused look on his face, Steven said, "I don't understand how an ambulance could be delayed two days in a row. Maybe this is intentional?"

"Well, we'll get to the bottom of it," Dr. Kolodney said.

The next morning everyone anxiously awaited the ambulance to arrive. *Something is wrong. I'm not going to be transferred. The ambulance isn't coming, is it?*

"I'll be back in a moment Kate," Steven said. "I need to call Dr. Kolodney. I'm going to find out why the ambulance hasn't arrived." He paged the doctor and sat waiting in the lounge.

"The ambulance isn't here and we have to get this done today or she may die from disappointment, literally. I fear she may give up her will to live. I am going to call over there now." Dr. Kolodney dialed the number to the admission office and handed the phone to Steven. I guess a good doctor knows when to get a good lawyer involved.

Speaking to admissions, Steven quickly became irate. "Here, you see if you can get a straight answer," he growled, handing the phone back to the doctor.

The doctor sounded frustrated and worried. "This woman needs to be transferred. Please send an ambulance now," he pleaded. Steven pulled out the verbal 2x4, grabbed the phone and started yelling, "Look! I know what is going on here. You are afraid I will sue you because I'm a lawyer. I will not sue anyone unless your ambulance does not come over here. If there is no ambulance within two hours then I will sue you. I will depose everyone who has ever worked at your hospital. You will all live in a courtroom until you are senile!"

This was a complete bluff on Steven's part. Luckily the admissions department did not have any attorneys working behind the desk.

"Look," Steven continued, "you can be afraid of being sued and that will get you sued for sure; or you can take a chance and treat a sick woman just like the Hippocratic Oath requires, and you may not get sued. The choice is yours." Steven then handed the phone back to the doctor who added his angry voice to the mix.

Two highly educated men yelling on the phone seemed to do the trick. It was finally decided that an ambulance would be sent for me that day.

From the Other Side of the Bed

T hings were more serious than Kate knew. Dr. Kolodney was convinced that Kate would not live out the day. In his opinion, if we could not do something to get her transferred, the battle would be over. They never had intended to admit her to Freeman Hospital. The rehab evaluation had been conducted before Kate had shown any real progress. What the evaluator said convinced the hospital that there was no potential whatsoever for Kate to recover.

I was so pushy and over the top that the staff had been afraid to tell me "No" because I simply would not hear it. So, instead of dealing with a crazy man, the case manager had appeased me by telling me that Kate would be accepted.

I don't know how it got from that point to the point where the hospital was lying to us about sending an

Paralyzed but not Powerless

ambulance. The act of lying put the hospital in an untenable position. It probably would have been okay for them to refuse Kate in the first place and stick to it, but by lying about it, they were now exposed to suit if something went wrong.

When I got on the phone with the admitting office, I made it very clear that the hospital was going to get sued if they did not come to get Kate – right now! One of the reasons they were not anxious to pick her up was because they feared I would sue them no matter what happened. I told them that if they kept operating out of fear they soon would realize their worst fear. If they wanted to avoid being sued, then the only safe course was to come and get Kate.

I yelled at them, then Dr. Kolodney yelled at them, then about two hours later, an ambulance arrived.

I can remember it as if it were yesterday. The ambulance drivers were scared out of their wits. They saw in front of their eyes a woman who was so fragile that they were not sure she could be safely transported. But they did it.

I think they fell in love with this fragile, determined woman, certainly they fell in love with her cause, because they came back several times to visit her in Rehab.

Everyone loves being part of a miracle.

I remember that Friday morning when I was transferred. Mum, Steven and a couple of friends were in my room. Two ambulance attendants came in. *Thank you God!* My prayer was answered. The men carefully transferred me onto a gurney and wheeled me downstairs cautiously while Steven held my hand. Gently, I was put into the ambulance. I found out later they were the same men who had taken me to the hospital at the onset of my stroke. "You'll be okay, Katie babes, I'm following right behind," Mum said. I still had tubes coming out of me everywhere. *Mum! Please don't leave me. I'm scared.*

"Don't worry, Kate, my name is Darryl and I'll be sitting with you back here" said one attendant. *Oh God, give me the strength to do therapy.*

Later, while in rehab, these two men visited me and said they had been just as scared about transferring me as I was. I had to be moved while I was still hooked up to IVs, a stomach tube and an oxygen tank. I was as frail as anyone they could remember transporting. I think they were afraid that I might break! I looked far more dead than alive that summer afternoon as our little band made its slow progression to the new hospital. I was in the ambulance, Steven's car followed, and a friend's car followed behind him. The whole thing was eerie, like a funeral procession. *Well, they say death is like a birth. Here we go again.*

The ride to the hospital took forever. I lay there, watching through the ambulance windows, my first real look at the world in a long time. *I can see trees. I wonder where we are?* Darryl constantly checked my vital signs and kept an oxygen mask on me. I began to panic. *I can't breathe.* Darryl realized my anxiety. "Take deep, slow breaths, Kate, we are almost there."

We arrived at Freeman Hospital without incident. Mum stayed with me while Steven went to the admissions office. *How long will I be here?* "This looks like a nice hospital, Kate," she said. I was lying on a gurney in the lobby and it did not appear as if anyone knew I was coming, nor did they know what to do with me now that I was there.

Steven did his best to solve the problem. Apparently there was no paperwork on my case. I waited and waited. *What if I get sent back to Torrance Memorial Hospital?* I banished the thought immediately.

It took about an hour and half before we left for the two-north-east wing which was set aside for spinal and brain injuries. The private room was small and plain with a wooden crucifix on the wall.

I was going to be spending three months at this hospital. Mum taped pictures the girls had drawn and some *Bible* verses on the wall. One of those verses was Isaiah 40:31, "But they that wait upon the Lord shall renew their strength; they shall mount up with wings as eagles; they shall run, and not be weary; and they shall walk, and not faint."

I held onto that idea with faith that I would walk again. Another verse was Philippians 4:13, "You can do all things through Christ who strengthens you." I would never give up hope that I would walk again. *I have come this far. Surely God will not abandon me now.*

That afternoon I met the team I would be working with. Because of the extent of brain damage I had suffered, I was placed on the spinal cord team. This was a team of people who primarily worked with quadriplegics. These patients did not usually walk again. I met my new neurologist, Dr. Alexander, who would be overseeing me during rehab. I remember feeling very scared. I fluctuated wildly between a positive eagerness to walk again, and bouts of depression that this was hopeless. *I don't want to meet a new team of people. I just want to go home.*

Different people popped in and out of my room. They included an occupational therapist, physical therapist, head nurse and dietician. The final person was Dr. Alexander. He asked my family to step outside while he did a quick assessment of my situation. I lay there while he looked me over from top to bottom. *I wonder what he is thinking. Does he think I will get better?*

Dr. Alexander seemed satisfied with what he saw. "Yes, I think this will work. We will first get rid of the catheter, then the trachea tube and finally the feeding tube. Kate, I think you will do well in rehab."

Those words of encouragement were what I needed to hear. That afternoon I met the 15-person team who would be working with me. *I can't believe how many people it takes to get the job done.*

Steven had a talk with Dr. Alexander. He found out that the hospital had not wanted to take me because the evaluation had been horribly negative. They had assessed me before I had regained any movement. The woman who had seen me in ICU saw a woman in a rigid fetal position with little sign of life.

Her original report had been that I had no potential for reha-bilitation. No one had bothered to inform the Freeman Hospital staff that I had made progress. Though small, my progress was significant. It proved that there was hope for recovery. Now I was in a place where I was going to get the best treatment possible. My team was dedicated and I had the support of my family.

It was now up to me.

Chapter Seven

~

Blocks in a Box

I remember the first morning of what would be intense therapy. It was a Monday. I was terrified and nervous. I had no idea what to expect. My first self-care session was with Joyce, the head nurse. It started with a sponge bath. This sponge bath was different than all the rest because it was going to require my participation.

Joyce didn't see me as a disabled person. She saw me as a person with disabilities. She was a bit abrasive though. Later I realized that her main job was to irritate me enough so that I would be determined to do things on my own.

She poked her head through my curtain then quickly disappeared saying, "I'll be back in five minutes." *What's going to happen now?* She returned with a bowl of warm water, a towel, wash cloth and a bar of soap. *Not the sponge bath! They have no idea how much that hurts. It's humiliating, I feel like a helpless baby.* My positive attitude lost altitude fast – over nothing really.

I started crying as Joyce approached me placing the items on the side table. In a stern voice she said, "We have no time for tears, Kate. We have work to do." *This woman should show some compassion. Look what I've been through!* "I know you are frightened, but crying isn't going to help. Save the tears for later Kate." *I can see crying around you won't help.* I decided that when Joyce approached me, I would hold back the tears no matter how difficult

93

that might be. Besides, I knew she was right. *I need to stay strong. Crying is not going to get me to walk again or get me home to the girls.*

Joyce elevated the bed, gently leaning me forward to remove my hospital gown. The cold air sent a chill down my spine. I couldn't resist, or even react. I could do nothing except be miserable. *You're not the one lying here. It's freezing!* Joyce laid me back down and nestled the washcloth in my hand. She put her hand over mine and began gently caressing my skin. "That's it Kate, follow along with me," she said. It was a slow process and I was freezing and in pain. I started crying again. *How is this going to help?*

We finished the sponge bath and she dried me. I felt helpless; my limp body was like a rag doll. She brought out a bra. *Why do you care if I am wearing a bra? I don't care if it all hangs out. I just care about getting my life back.*

Joyce leaned me forward, steadying me with one hand, and with the other pulled the bra straps onto my shoulders and snapped the hook in the back. *Okay, now she has my attention. I know how good some men are at the one-handed bra technique when it comes to taking it off. I didn't know there was a one-handed technique to putting it on.* My mental attitude took a sudden upturn. Little did I know that the one handed technique would be a key to my future success as a speaker.

Next, Joyce helped me with the T-shirt. She reached for a clean diaper and slid it under me, pulling the adhesive tabs at the sides, fitting it snugly on my hips. "This is only temporary Kate, until you learn bladder control," she reassured me. *What? I hope that comes back. Well I know this is a rebirth – but a diaper?*

This was the first time in a long while I hadn't worn a hospital gown. It felt bizarre. *I'm actually wearing real clothes!* She pulled the elastic waist shorts on and the final step to dressing was the "Ted hose." *What are those ugly things?*

"Everyone has to wear these Kate, to help with the circulation and prevent blood clots," Joyce said as she struggled to pull them on. *These are hideous. Well at least they definitely won't run!*

Tennis shoes were placed on my feet, and I was ready for therapy. I certainly wasn't making a fashion statement. *I don't care what I look like. I just want to get better.* I was about to learn the enormity of the task ahead, and the emotional stamina that recovery requires.

My therapists put me on a grueling schedule from 9 a.m. until 3 p.m. I had no energy nor endurance. I was pretty much a prisoner in my body, still almost completely paralyzed. I couldn't even move my fingers enough to activate the call button for a nurse. I was totally alone. Panic overcame me. *How am I ever going to get my life back? I am willing to do whatever it takes. It's the only chance I have.*

My second day in rehab continued like an endless SAT examination. Therapist after therapist came and went. Mum sat with me through it all.

One of the first people I remember was an occupational therapist who bustled into my room carrying a small black box and a clipboard. *Who is this woman and what is that she is carrying?* The woman was petite with short, cropped blonde hair. "Hi I'm Katrina from occupational therapy. I just need to do an evaluation on Kate," she said.

Mum got up out of the chair. "I'll come back after you are finished," she said. "No, no that's fine. I won't be long," the therapist said.

Katrina opened the box explaining that she was going to test my joint range of motion. "We need to make sure that's normal," she said. Taking a safety pin, she began pricking my skin in various areas. "Close your eyes Kate, and tell me if you feel this," she said. *Ouch! Of course, I can feel that! But how I am I supposed to tell you?* "Some stroke survivors lose sense of touch," she said while taking notes of my reactions.

She also tested my muscle strength by having me squeeze a gadget called a dynamometer. "Now Kate, take this in your right hand and squeeze as hard as you can." I squeezed with every ounce of energy I had. "Really squeeze," Katrina said. *I'm squeezing! I'm squeezing!* "Good Kate, I can tell we have some strength there to build on."

From the Other Side of the Bed

*W*hy, when you have two people in the hospital with nearly identical injuries, does one make it and the other does not.

What is that quality that allows one person to go that extra mile?

I call it the human element and Kate had it in spades. It wasn't just stubbornness. Kate had scheduled one hour workouts on the mat in the gym two or three times a day. These workouts were her chance to get better. Usually, out of that hour, a good fifteen minutes was spent getting the patient from the room to the gym, then getting ready to work out and not working out. But that isn't how it was with Kate.

Kate didn't wait for someone to come for her. She had me push the wheelchair there early so that when the hour started she could use the whole hour to work out. When she was further along she would push herself to the gym.

Where does that drive come from? It's a gift I think, It's like the gift of faith. It is given to us when we most need it. It is a creation of grace or maybe just good old fashioned stubbornness.

Days passed. I was making progress. The lid to the glass coffin had finally shattered and I was coming into the land of the living. One day, in walks Katrina with that little black wooden box. "Now let's test your dexterity," she said cheerfully. She raised the head of the bed, sitting me up. She took an assortment of colored blocks out of the box and started to arrange them on the bed table. *What's going to happen now?* "This particular exercise will give me an idea of your gross motor coordination," she said. *What is gross motor coordination?* "What I'd like you to do is try to pick up each block and place it in the empty side of the box," she explained. *Blocks in a box. Seems simple enough.*

"I'm going to give you a minute to see how many blocks you can get in there," she said. Katrina looked into my eyes for a signal. "Ready?" *Yeah, I'm ready.* I fumbled with the blocks.

"Come on, Katie, you can do this," Mum said encouragingly. *I'm trying.*

"Okay, I think that's good," Katrina said, taking some notes. I started to cry. *I can't even put blocks in a box.* "You did fine Kate, don't cry," the therapist said.

Mum in a stern voice, said, "Come on, you can do this. Pull yourself together. You have to get through this."

Another therapist stopped by to do some evaluations. She introduced herself as Delia, and said she was going to be my Physical Therapist. Delia was young and pretty with long hair tied back in a ponytail. *She's seems too young to be doing this kind of work. It's not fair that she gets to go home at night while I'm stuck here!* "I'm just going to test lower body strength in your legs," she said. I followed her instructions as she took notes. After her thirty minute evaluation she left me to rest. Though my attitude was a little negative at this point, I was eager to begin therapy.

There was a knock at my door. "Hi Kate," announced a friendly voice. Then I saw this tall slender woman, mid-50s, standing at the foot of my bed. Her head was a mass of tight curls and her smile stretched from ear to ear. She was matronly looking, dressed in a navy skirt, a white shirt with a buttoned down collar and a navy sweater. *Oh, no, a nun! She's going to try and convert me!*

She held a folder full of papers under her arm as she came closer to the bedside. "I'm Sister Delores," she said in a soft voice. "I'll be visiting you for a few minutes each day. I visit all the patients in the ward so you'll be seeing a lot of me."

I just gazed up at her in wonder. *How can she keep smiling and talk at the same time?* The Sister touched my arm. "I know how hard it is dear, but you mustn't give up. You have those two beautiful babies to get home to." She reached over me and picked up the photo of my daughters. "Oh my, what beautiful girls." *I'm trying to choke back the tears.* Of course, right on cue, I started to cry. *Why did God let this happen?*

"Oh Honey, it's okay to cry. It's very normal, Kate. That's part of the stroke process." Sister Delores said. *She's way too sweet and nice.*

Tears were flowing down my cheeks. She leaned closer to my face and squeezed my hand. "Remember Kate, baby steps. God is always with you. He won't forsake you." I looked into her eyes. *If God is so great, why did this happen? Where is He now?*

She placed a little prayer card on the shelf beside me. It was the Lord's Prayer. "I'll see you tomorrow, dear. I have to go now." She turned and left the room. Her few words had been encouraging to me. God's word was what I needed to hear and to be reminded that I would heal and should lean on Him.

From the Other Side of the Bed

We are not Catholics, but people of faith have a common bond, a universal bond. Wait a minute, isn't that what catholic means? "Having sympathies with all." Well, Sister Delores certainly exemplified that.

I was very glad the hospital was a Catholic hospital. God and faith were spoken here. I know that Kate now had a whole religious order praying for her.

Though I wasn't able to speak, Sister Delores was always there to comfort me and hold my hand. She understood everything I said, even though I only spoke with my eyes.

She seemed to understand that this adversity was deepening my relationship with God. I had been stripped of everything and He was re-building a new Kate. I didn't understand it then, but the emotional see-saw was part of the process. *I know God has plans for me. I feel so down. I am so devastated. Why me? I can't even talk. What have I done to deserve this?*

All through this ordeal, I had been afraid to be alone. For some reason, as I got better the fear of being alone got worse. At night especially, I was terrified. It had been reassuring in ICU to have someone sit with me all night. Here in the Freeman Hospital I was by myself. Steven understood my fear and spoke with Amy. The evening nurses were notified to play soft music continually in my room. Steven sat with me in the evenings, never leaving until I fell asleep. He went to the nurse's station every night at 9 p.m. to remind them to administer my sleeping medication. He then waited until the medication took effect before leaving.

I hated nights. I often woke up in the middle of the night with the urge to urinate. The catheter had been the first thing to go upon arrival at Freeman Hospital. Learning bladder control was a goal. As a precaution, I wore diapers but I was supposed to call for a nurse whenever I felt the urge to go to the bathroom.

It was next to impossible to push the nurse's call button. One evening, I tried buzzing the nurse's station. "Ye – ssss?" emanated from the intercom. She sounded a little irritated. I looked anxiously toward the door waiting for the nurse. Answering back would have been nice but I couldn't utter a word! Using all my strength, I tried again.

"Yessss?" came through the intercom. Frustrated, I wanted to scream. *Look at the chart, I've had a stroke. I can't speak!*

From the Other Side of the Bed

*K*ate and I had a running gag. When we wanted privacy we would push the call button for the nurse. In intensive care Kate had one nurse she shared with only one other patient. Here in Rehab, she shared one nurse with ten or more patients.

I kept pushing the button. *Please come here. I need help!*

Finally, the nurse appeared. "Do you need something?" she asked. *Obviously, I need something or I wouldn't keep pushing the button. I needed you five minutes ago. Now it's a little late.* The damage was done.

"Do you need the bedpan?" she asked. Walking toward my bed, she grabbed it off the shelf. *It's a little late for that.* Pulling back the covers, she realized what I had been trying to communicate. She let out a heavy sigh, as if I had created extra work for her, which I had. But whose fault was that? I felt embarrassed, like a small child being scolded.

Gradually, over time, I regained bladder control. The diapers were only worn at night as a precaution. Having had three or four bladder infections while in the hospital, it was tough learning bladder control. The feeling I had of constantly needing to go to the bathroom, and nothing happening, drove the nurses crazy. Learning bladder control reminded me of potty training my own daughter. Here I was, learning the basics of life all over again; diapers, potty training. Sometimes when God makes you into a new person, He starts at the very beginning!

I was transferred into a wheelchair that first week. Delia, my physical therapist, assisted Katrina. After my self-care session with Joyce every morning, I lay on my bed resting. Just about the time I finished my self-care, Steven would walk in. He always made an effort to act as if he was in a much better mood than he was.

The therapist walked in mid-morning, pushing a massive wheelchair. *I'm not going anywhere in that thing!* "Hi Kate, we are going to sit you up in a wheelchair and take you on a tour of the hospital floor," Katrina said. *I don't want a tour. I am fine right here.* But, when you can't speak you don't have a choice.

The two of them gently transferred me into the wheelchair. *I hate it that I can't say anything!* My body was weak and I had no trunk control. Katrina situated me in the chair, placing a pillow behind my head for support. It had a huge back that reclined. She secured a strap across my stomach and snapped it in place. *What a hassle for a tour I don't want.*

"If you feel ill from sitting in this position, we can recline the chair," Katrina said, pushing the wheelchair out the door. Delia followed with the portable tank of oxygen. Steven trailed behind us.

I feel sick. I started crying.

"Oh no, she is crying, Delia," Katrina said concerned.

"Don't cry Kate. It will get better," Delia said.

This was my first tour of the unit. We passed by the therapist's board schedules and the nurse's station. "Now we are going to go and see the apartment," Katrina said. *An apartment? What is an apartment doing in a hospital?* I was wheeled down the hallway to a door that opened to a set of rooms that resembled an apartment.

As we entered into the main room, I noticed a couch, chairs and coffee table in one corner. In another corner was a small open kitchen with all the amenities.

"Each week we have a cooking class where patients can learn to cook again," Katrina explained. There was a dining area complete with a large table surrounded with chairs. "This is something you'll be doing while in rehabilitation," she said. *I don't want to learn to cook.*

"Kate never cooked prior to the stroke," Steven said laughing. Both therapists laughed with him.

"Well, Kate, I can promise you they won't be gourmet meals, but you'll learn some neat tricks in the kitchen," Katrina said.

I noticed a washing machine and dryer against the wall. "Kate, here is where patients can learn to do their own laundry from their wheelchairs," Katrina said wheeling me over to the equipment. *What? Do my own laundry? From a wheelchair? I just want my life back. I plan on walking out of here.*

Katrina pushed the wheelchair into a room where there was a king-sized bed. "The bed is used for patients to practice rolling over and getting out of bed," she said. *I have to learn that too?*

"Upon discharge, patients are given the option of staying over night alone in the apartment, or with their spouse, to feel what life is going to be like once they are home again. Located all around the apartment are emergency cords to pull if a patient needs help," she reassured me. *I cannot imagine spending the night in that room with Steven. Who would roll him out of bed in the morning?* She wheeled me into a large bathroom off to the side. I had never seen so many devices in a bathroom.

I know you both mean well, but it is discouraging to think about having to relearn everything again. I felt as if someone had thrown a dark blanket of sadness over me. I tried to hold back my tears, but I had already started to cry, which quickly turned into a wail.

Steven said, "It's okay to cry, Honey. Let the tears come."

"This is a part of the mourning process," Delia said. *I can't do this! I didn't plan on life turning out this way.* I continued sobbing as the therapists wheeled me back to my room, now a safe haven for me. *Why did they have to show me that?*

Steven and Mum were with me for my first therapy session. A therapist named Kelly wheeled me to a gym. Looking back, her jovial attitude was commendable. At the same time, it wasn't going to make me walk or talk again. *I wish this whole ordeal were over. I'm scared. I feel dizzy sitting up. This is enough work just getting in this wheelchair!*

"It's okay, Kate. Everyone is nervous about therapy in the beginning," Kelly said.

"Come on, Katie babes, pull yourself together. You can do this," Mum said.

Easy for you to say, but I'm the one having to do it. I could feel my heart racing with anticipation, and a lot of fear. *What will I be doing?*

"Our session will last 30 minutes and then I'll get you back to bed to rest," Kelly said. She wheeled the chair to the edge of the mat. I glanced out the window at the sunny blue sky. I had no choice but to try and follow her instructions. *If only this were a dream and none of this was happening. God, please give me the strength to get through this.*

I don't recall any details of that first therapy session, but I do remember feeling overwhelmed and fatigued. *I'm exhausted. I can't even perform these simple exercises. This feels hopeless! When is this double vision going to dissipate? Why does my face feel numb on one side? I wish I could ask questions. I wish I had answers. I just want to feel better.*

Halfway through my session Mum realized how damp my shirt had become. "Kate, your shirt is saturated," she said alarmed. *Yes, I know. This is sitting up for you, for me it is a workout. I feel like I have run a marathon.* "I'm going to get you a clean shirt. I don't want you catching cold," Mum said concerned.

Mum, I don't need a clean shirt.

"Good idea. It's amazing the energy it takes for her to just sit up," Kelly said. Mum returned and Kelly assisted her in changing my shirt. After returning to my room, I lay on my bed feeling angry and depressed. *I can't even change my own clothes. I can't do anything.*

Later that day, Mum told Joyce that she was worried that I wasn't getting enough rest and asked about limiting the visitors.

"I'm going to be gone soon and I want to spend as much time as I can with you," she said. "You don't need all these visitors wearing you out."

Steven disagreed, but was too tired to fight with his mother-in-law, so we adopted her rules.

It was decided I would be placed on an up and down schedule allowing me some rest. This meant after the self-care session with Katrina, I would rest before my next therapy session. Visitors were limited to ten minutes a day, and only after 3 p.m. I enjoyed seeing people, but Mum was right – the visits were draining my energy.

My friend, Jenny, was there the next afternoon for a session of my therapy. She had previously asked Katrina if she could watch. Jenny pushed my chair as Katrina walked beside me. We headed to one of three mat rooms.

Katrina wheeled my chair to the edge of the mat platform and set the brakes. Then she helped me up onto the mat. *I feel like a rag doll.* The platform was a wooden frame with a comfortably padded vinyl-coated nylon covering. It was a couple of feet off the ground so the patient could easily transfer from a wheelchair.

Katrina urged me to sit near the edge, placing both feet on the ground for weight bearing. *What if I fall?* "Kate, try lifting your right hip and move toward the edge. Now try lifting your left hip and do the same," she said encouragingly.

I remembered what Sister Delores told me, "Everything is a baby step." *God, give me the strength to do this.*

Katrina's goal was to help me constantly increase the highest level of independence and to apply it to my daily living. "We need to work on your trunk control and strength," she said. "It's the most important asset you have to work with at this point."

She produced some plastic stacking cones. "Sit up straight and squeeze your shoulder blades," Katrina said. "Okay Jenny, stand in front of Kate and hold the small end of the cone toward her." Katrina had me visualize grasping a yellow cone and pulling it out of Jenny's hand. *Okay, that makes sense.*

Meanwhile, Katrina laid my left hand flat at my side on the mat pushing so it became weight bearing. "Try to put weight through this hand," she said. *How can I remember all this stuff?*

It was overwhelming to try to think of so many things at once. Katrina sat beside me, watching my trunk control.

"That's it Katie. Great job, praise God!" Jenny cheered enthusiastically.

This seemingly simple task was extremely difficult and took all my energy. *How can I be this weak?* We tried this for about fifteen minutes before moving onto another exercise. Katrina sat a slightly tilted stool beside me. My hand was placed flat on the top of a piece of royal blue, sticky material. The material, Dycem, helped secure my hand. This was something the therapists used a lot. Katrina instructed me to try pushing with my left hand while keeping my back upright, shoulder blades squeezed. This took all of my concentration.

The session lasted no longer than thirty minutes but it left me completely exhausted. Katrina transferred me back into the wheelchair, and we headed to my room. "Good job Katie," Jenny said. *You have no idea how hard that was!*

Jenny stayed in my room keeping me company while I rested. It helped to have a friend there. She had been a good friend, spending numerous afternoons with me in ICU. She had a maternal demeanor, a zeal for life and a love for Jesus. I was hoping God would answer her prayers and give me another miracle. Some great leap forward.

"It's so beautiful outside. We need to get you up, Katie, and take a tour in your wheelchair," she cheerfully said. *Are you sure we should do this? I guess you know what you are doing.* Her mother was a stroke survivor in a wheelchair, so I felt comfortable with her.

Jenny sat me on the edge of the bed steadying me as she swung my legs around lifting me into the wheelchair. She propped my feet on each footrest. "Katie, we are ready," she said as she pushed me out into the hallway toward the nurse's station where she checked me out like a book at the library.

She wheeled me to the elevator which we took to the first floor, then out into the parking lot. *She's right, what a beautiful day. The sun feels good on my face. It feels wonderful to be outside in the fresh air. How I have missed the warm summer days.* I appreciated seeing the tall trees and plants bursting with color and life.

We headed down the path toward the hospital health center. Many emotions stirred up inside me as I viewed the hospital health center. It reminded me of once being fit and healthy, able to work out. It had been a big part of my life. Now, I was stuck in a wheelchair. I started crying.

Jenny leaned over and began wiping my tears on her skirt. She turned the wheelchair and started to head back, "Now Katie, that's a true friend when you can wipe your tears on her skirt." Jenny's visits stopped with Mum's plan of limiting the visitors. I missed her terribly.

Dr. Jeffrey Saver's Comments:

$\mathcal{R}$ecovery from a stroke occurs as intact parts of the brain take over the functions of the damaged parts, to the extent they are able to do so. Recent brain imaging studies have disclosed that this shift in functional activity begins soon after a stroke, and is driven by training and practice. This activity-dependent neuroplasticity is the biological substrate of successful rehabilitation.

Learning to control even simple movements, and tasks, is an extraordinary challenge to portions of an adult nervous system already committed to other functions. In Kate's case, her youth and excellent fitness before the stroke were factors favoring a good recovery, despite the severe brain injury she suffered. Most important were her spirit and determination. In the crucible of rehabilitation, stroke survivors become stroke victors.

Stephanie's rendering of *Kate's Journey.*

Rachel's illustration of Kate, drawn when she was age five.

Chapter Eight

~

Settling In

$\mathcal{A}$my explained her role as a social worker. "Kate, I'm here if you need to discuss any issues," she reassured me. *I just need physical therapy; I don't need psychological help.* Or so I thought.

"I think it would be good for Kate to see her daughters every day. How have they adjusted with her absence?" Amy asked Steven. *See my daughters? No, I don't want to until I'm better. You know what happened last time. I don't want them to see me like this.*

"It's been very difficult for them," Steven said.

Amy expressed the importance for the girls to see that I was okay. "You will have a life again, Kate, and you'll do many activities with the girls," she said. *What kind of life? What can I do with my kids? I am paralyzed!*

"Kate, I have a daughter about Rachel's age, and I can imagine what you must be going through not able to see them," Amy said. *No, you can't!* I started to cry. "I'll try to help you as much as I can," she reassured me. *Try to help? What can you possibly do? I just want to get on the floor and play with them like other mothers.*

"I think when the girls come to visit, it would be good to have a bag of toys here at the hospital. They can play and visit with Kate," Amy said.

"That's a terrific idea, I'll pick up some things today," Mum said.

"Kate, you are going to feel like you are on a roller coaster with your emotions. Every stroke patient has a difficult time controlling them. This is normal," Amy explained. *Control my emotions? My life has been turned upside down.*

Amy mentioned that I would probably get close to a couple of the team members during my stay at Freeman Hospital. *There's no way. I have no desire to make friends. I just want to work hard and walk out of here.*

Family members were encouraged to visit. It was decided my daughters would visit me for an hour each day after therapy. I'll never forget the first time Rachel came to see me. Mum asked the nurse to sit me up in the wheelchair. The nurse tried to camouflage the trachea tube by tucking it under my hospital gown. A pillow was propped behind my neck. Mum brushed my hair, letting it flow onto my shoulders. "There you go, Katie babes," she said.

Amy was seated in the room when the girls arrived. Amanda (the nanny) stood in the doorway holding Rachel with Stephanie beside her. She bent down, "There Rachel, go say hi to Mom," she said. Rachel held on to Amanda's leg and started to cry. "Mommy, Mommy, pick me up." *Rachel I'm your mum, not Amanda. She doesn't even remember me!*

"Stephanie why don't you bring Rachel over to her mom?" suggested Amy. I started to cry. "Don't cry, Mom," she said, taking Rachel by the hand and coming toward me.

Rachel refused to come too close. She held onto Stephanie's hand. "Sissy, sissy," she said.

"It's okay, Rachel, it's Mom," Stephanie replied.

The wheelchair frightened her. *Stephanie is so grown up, taking care of her sister and comforting me. I love you girls very much. I miss you.*

After some time the girls got used to me. Stephanie and Rachel sat on my bed coloring. "Look, Mom, I'm coloring a picture for your room. Do you want to help me color?" Stephanie asked.

"Your mom can't do that yet," Amy said. *No, I can't color in the lines.*

Amanda didn't stay long and was preparing the girls to leave. Rachel reached out and handed me a crayon but kept her distance. *Thanks, Honey; I will hold your crayon; wish I could hold you.* The girls left.

"I think it would be a good idea if I got a grounds pass for Kate so the girls can visit her outside. That will be a less threatening environment," Amy said.

Everyone agreed. *I don't want to see the girls until I'm better. I feel so helpless. I couldn't even help Stephanie do a simple thing like coloring.*

Slowly, it did get better. From that point on, the highlight of my day was when my daughters came to visit. Amy got a grounds pass and I spent an hour visiting the girls each afternoon. Steven and Mum wheeled me downstairs where I would meet the girls and the nanny in the park. We sat under the shade of a huge oak tree. My dominating thought on these beautiful days was what if I couldn't get to a toilet in time!

From my wheelchair I'd sit and watch the girls run up and down the grassy bank. *They aren't even interested in me sitting here, but I suppose it shows them I am still alive.*

From the Other Side of the Bed

*K*ate worked as hard as any human being could and she would have burned out if she did not take a break. For Kate, that break was visiting the park with her children.

One reason Kate had fought as hard as she did, was because she wanted to be a mother. It was the single most important thing in her life. So we made sure that each day she had time in the park with her girls. It was Kate's reward and motivation to do her therapy.

At first it was heartbreaking, because Rachel would not come to her mother. She was still a toddler and was confused by all that was happening. As the months passed, she had adopted the nanny as her mother.

It tore Kate apart to see another woman driving her new car and wearing her clothes (something I did not even notice). The worst, was having her baby call another woman Mommy.

Happily, as time passed, and Rachel got to spend more time with Kate, she accepted Kate as her real mum. The visits to the park were the high points of Kate's day. She would sit in her wheelchair, and watch the children play.

Mum tried taking my mind off the stroke by talking about other things. She loosened my hair out of the braid and let the air get to it. I just listened as she talked. She seemed to be able to read my mind. "You can't always think about your stroke. You need to take an interest in what the kids are doing," she said. My thoughts shifted from positive, to negative, to irrelevant. *It's hard not to think about it. I just want to walk again. I can't think about anything else.*

From the Other Side of the Bed

I never left Kate until she was asleep – sometime between 11 p.m. and 3 a.m. Some nights were easier than others. I would often have to hold her legs down so they wouldn't shake.

I bought some books on tape and Kate and I would listen to them until she fell asleep. We went though the entire Chronicles of Narnia as read by Anthony Hopkins. I still love those books. When we finished reading, I would put on worship music, which I left softly playing all night.

We also had the Bible on tape and listened to Charlton Heston's rich voice reading the New Testament, night after night. Kate said that Charlton Heston was better than Ambien!

On my first afternoon in the park, I was sitting watching the girls, when Rachel came up to me and angrily scratched my arm. *Rachel, that's not nice to scratch your mum. Honey, I know you are angry with me for leaving you. I didn't want to.*

Mum discussed this with Amy at my next visit. "I think it would be good if Kate could transfer from the wheelchair onto the bench, so Rachel will feel more comfortable," Amy said. *What's the point? Rachel doesn't see me as her mother. She is angry with me.*

Amy's suggestion worked well. When the girls came to visit me in the park the next time, Mum had placed some snacks in my lap. This encouraged Rachel to come over to me. At first she was reluctant. She was afraid of the wheelchair, which was sitting near me. It was scary to a toddler. But, over time, we reestablished our mother-daughter relationship.

My butt ached constantly from all the sitting, so Steven would help me stand.

"Do you think you should be standing like that without a therapist?" Mum asked.

"Yes," I managed to get out. *Mum if you had to sit all day in a wheelchair, your butt would ache too! I just need to relieve the pain.*

It felt good, as I stood with my arm wrapped around Steven's neck. Mum rubbed my bottom (you can imagine that scene). I wanted to keep standing, but my legs would buckle under me, forcing me to sit back in the wheelchair.

It broke my heart that Rachel thought Amanda was her mother. It bothered me to watch Amanda driving around in my brand new Jeep. Steven had bought it for me just a week before my stroke, and now some stranger was driving my kids around in it. The car wasn't new anymore.

Amanda was even wearing my clothes. It made me sad and jealous. When she brought a Victoria's Secret clothing catalogue for me to look at, it made me more depressed. *What the heck is she thinking?* There were times I would just sit and cry about it. No one really understood. I was too confused, embarrassed and humiliated to explain my feelings, even had I been able to.

I began to look forward to my time in the park after a day spent in therapy. The park was real life; an oasis in the bleak world of pain and tears that was the routine of my day. It was peaceful, sitting on a bench or in my chair, with small fragments of sunlight shining through the trees and warming me. One day, I sat for the entire time just watching a small squirrel scurrying about, busily doing squirrel errands amongst the branches of the tree I was under. I began to look forward to seeing that squirrel every day. The kids would leave some little bit of their snack for my little furry tree dweller.

Every day the squirrel would venture down the tree to see what we had left for him. I was jealous of that little guy. I yearned for the day when I would have that kind of freedom.

I was so committed to therapy that I would wheel myself to the gym just to get five minutes extra therapy. I had trained for years, five days a week, and I brought that same intensity to my rehabilitation. I thank God I was never a couch potato prior to the stroke, or I may never have had the freedom I enjoy today.

Amy suggested to my family that I start keeping a journal. *How will that help? How am I supposed to write in a journal?*

"What a great idea, Kate. I'll bring one in for you," said Mum. At first Steven and my mother made the entries. They were simple entries, logging my daily therapy. Eventually Amy suggested I start writing in the journal myself. Some of those entries are in this book, so you can see my early stages of learning to write again. I was right-handed and since my right hand had regained some motion and dexterity, it meant I just needed to gain my strength back. By writing a few minutes each day, thankfully I did.

At the time I didn't feel as if I was making any progress. But looking back over my journal, I am amazed at how far I came, and how quickly. Today I appreciate that I was blessed with a miracle.

8- 10

UPGRADE   PILET

TO   SOFT

did test ~~spo que~~

more standing

Leqning on elbows

Kate Kuqnos

8-11

Stevens birthday
took some staps
knelt on knees
wheelchair mobility
~~sscending~~
writing
Lucy ~~g~~ncag

Kofe schlyaman
1210 8th st
mb
cal 9026

8-19

it's saturday and
very quiet
i dont like the
weekend

i pray for a mirol
on my left eye

did some more
stoping transfers
and went to the
park w/ kids
had dinne
or a reg
diet
think liquids

hard workout
took more
steps
worked on
keeping
shoulders back
tube
wound good

8 | 2 ?

much easier to
get dressed
put bra and shirt
on by myself
did a looking cluss
and ate the lunch
fett alfredo, bread
rolls, and choc
mousse pie

felt tired today
my muscles are sore
have to have help
always for to let

9-2
had accident in the
toilet. Steven forgot
to pull my pants
down. We laughed so
hard
9-2
had my shower
then worked out for
an 1½ with Derek
DD some am work
There is movement in
my elbow and
bicep. saw Sharon &
Roah with everyone
in the park.
had dinner
and rested.
some vistors
Barney
Terry
Jenny
Still weak on left
side but each
day is better

9-14

I took my shower &
went swimming first
which went really
well. I was able to handle
myself better. I then did
some PT with Delia and
showed Steven some
steps. It was then time
for lunch. I was late &
as usual the last to finish.
But I then had ot at 1pm
where I went down to out
patient and did some arm
and a little standing.
nina helped me with that.
It was a good session
I came back & had a 30
minute rest before heading
to pt at 2.30 which I did
stretching and leg
movements. Finally at 3pm
I rested then the
kids came and we
went to the park
with cheryl

10-6

Its Friday and I have
one more week here. I
cant wait to leave,
they have alot of
patients and not really
that much time for
me. It seems I'm too
healthy now!
I was suppose to have
swimming - I got ready
and Candice didnt show.
Then I got really upset
beause I couldnt get a
nurse to help me. They
were too busy. Denise
my nurse helped me to
shower and I worked
on the arm for an
hour. Candice came to
apologise. I did therapy
and then lunch.
After I lay down for
an hour and rested.
I then did some more
therapy until 3pm

I had to relearn everything – swallowing, speaking, sitting on the edge of the bed, transferring to a wheelchair and walking. Many of the simple things we take for granted were extremely difficult challenges for me. One session Delia and Katrina brought to me a funny looking plastic device. "This is called an Incentive Spirometer," Delia said. *What the heck is that?* "It will increase your ability to take bigger, deeper breaths."

"Using the Spirometer will also keep your lungs strong," Katrina added.

Delia told me to blow into the tube. *I don't want to blow into that thing!* "Go ahead Kate, try blowing while I hold it for you," she said. I started to laugh nervously sputtering my efforts to blow through the tube. *This is stupid. I can't do this with you watching.* Both therapists waited patiently for me to stop laughing. Delia held the device as I tried to blow into the tube. Nothing happened.

"Take a deep breath and try blowing as hard as you can," Katrina said. *See. I can't do it.* Katrina and Delia glanced at each other. "Really try to force some air into the tube," Delia said. I tried again. This time the tiny ball on the gauge moved – it barely moved, but it moved. I was beginning to feel light-headed from trying.

"I think you are exhausted from trying," Katrina said. "We will leave this with you. Try to practice as often as you can. You moved it to two hundred fifty. That's good. Our goal is for you to be able to move the ball to the 1,500 level, which is normal for a woman's breath," Delia said. *I'll never be able to do that.*

"I want you to try and do this every hour for a couple of minutes," Delia suggested. "Practice at night while watching television during the commercials." *Yes, that's something I could manage. I can see that I'm going to have to make it a priority.*

"This is something you can do on your own," Katrina said.

"It's not a part of your scheduled therapy, so remember to pace yourself," Delia said.

"As you breathe in, try to increase the length and strength of each breath. In order for you to speak again, we need to increase your lung capacity," Katrina said.

I persistently practiced when I could. I didn't rest. I constantly thought about breathing into the tube. *I have to do this or I'll never speak again.* Gradually my efforts paid off.

I remember the luxury of my first shower. *When is Katrina going to let me take a shower? I need to have my hair shampooed. My head itches.* "Can't we let Kate take a shower?" Steven asked.

"Well, I'm concerned about her open wounds, the trachea and the feeding tube," Katrina said, "but I'll check with her doctor." *I would love to take a real shower.* From the sponge baths, I had advanced to sitting on the edge of the bed with Katrina supporting my trunk.

She finally had me advance to doing my self-care from the wheelchair at the sink in my room. This was a painfully slow process.

As soon as my sitting balance was good enough, I was allowed to start taking showers. After my self-care session one morning we did a dry run as she called it.

She wanted to see if I could accomplish the transfer from the wheelchair onto the shower bench in the bathroom. "This is just practice. I want to make sure we have a safe environment that will allow enough time for the shower," Katrina said. *Safe environment?* She wheeled me into the spacious bathroom, bringing the chair close to the edge of the shower.

After setting the brakes, she said, "Now, there's a 3-inch ledge you'll have to step over, but for now I'm going to help you scoot onto the shower bench." *Three inches for her; Mt. Everest for me!*

Lifting the armrest on the wheelchair, she supported me onto the bench. Swinging my legs around, she scooted my body over. *Wow! This thing has a back support.* "I think this will be fine," she said. *I'm sad I can't take a shower today. I have been waiting for a long time.*

The next morning, Katrina came in with some tape and plastic. "We will be showering this morning; however, we need to cover your trachea and feeding tube with plastic." She cut pieces of plastic and taped them over the wound sites. *What a production.* Then she supported my transfer into the wheelchair. Before wheeling me into the bathroom, she put my tennis shoes on. *I need Nikes to move eighteen inches?*

In the bathroom, she brought my chair to the edge of the shower ledge. We went through the process we had practiced the day before. Katrina carefully scooted my body onto the bench bringing my legs around. She removed my shoes and gown.

"Try to keep your left arm in weight bearing. We need to place your left hand in position so your arm won't hang. This puts weight through the arm and activates the muscles," she said. *Just taking a shower is a therapy workout.* She pulled the curtain, and turned on the water.

The warm water sprayed on my body. *I'm finally taking a shower! Oh, this feels hea-ven-ly.* I had never felt so grateful for something as simple as a shower. I didn't want it to end. Tears of joy flowed down my cheeks. I felt embarrassed, hoping the tears would look like water from the shower. No such luck. Katrina was observant. She gently reassured me, "Crying at odd moments is a normal result of a stroke,"It will happen and there's no way for you to control it. Besides, this time there is a good reason to cry. It must feel wonderful taking your first shower." Taking the hand-held shower, Katrina wet my hair and began to lather shampoo into my scalp. *That feels good, but how am I going to do this myself with one hand?*

"Okay, Kate, I think we had better finish here in a moment. I don't want you to get tired from the hot water and steam," she said. She turned off the water and dried me while I sat on the bench. Carefully she dried my feet and put my shoes on. "I don't want you to slip," she said, laying what looked like about three dozen thick white towels on the floor. *Tennis shoes and nothing else but a head wrap. I must look a sight!*

Loosely covering me with a gown, she transferred me into my chair and dressed me.

Katrina explained the technique I'd be using for dressing. "Remember, Kate, as you dress you will cross your weak leg over your good leg." *I have to remind myself of that too? How am I going do all of this?* "As you undress, you have to reverse the process. Start with the weak side of your body," she said. *How am I going to remember everything?* Katrina assured me it would get easier. "This is as hard as it's going to be," she said, "Remember, as you are getting dressed we want your arm weight bearing and not just in your lap."

Weight bearing meant that my hand would support my body, thus allowing me to learn to balance myself. In a sense, you could say that weight bearing was the key to my new life!

From the Other Side of the Bed

I made friends with a very special man, a male nurse, Ron. He joined in a conspiracy to get Kate the best possible treatment.

Late, one night Ron came and got me. He told me that a special air mattress had just become available because of the discharge of a patient, actually I think someone died.

We sneaked into the room and stole the entire bed. We rolled the bed down the hall and into Kate's room. We quickly transferred Kate, who was trying not to laugh her head off, to the new bed, then returned the old bed without the staff being the wiser.

I suppose Ron could have been fired for helping me with such covert activities, but he wanted to do something to make Kate's situation a little more bearable.

Ron was wonderful. He looked like an escapee from Alcatraz. He had long hair, two long braids, more tattoos than an African warrior and a sense of humor that wouldn't quit. He came in every night, put on her hand

*splints, so her hands didn't clench in the night and set up
her pillows and bed so that she could sleep comfortably.*

*Occasionally, he would come in on days he was not
working. As I said, everyone wants to be part of a miracle.
Ron was a miracle in and of himself.*

"I think you are ready for a new wheelchair, Kate," Delia said.
As we turned the corner, I saw a row of wheelchairs lined up. Delia
walked down the row looking for the right one for me. I felt like I
was being fitted for a pair of shoes. Unlocking the chain she pulled
one from the line, "I think this will work."

The wheelchair was smaller than what I had, with no
headrest. The brand was *Quickie,* and it was lighter and easier to
manage than the old bulky one. It was comfortable, with a
cushioned seat and back. We wheeled toward the mat room. *This
will work. I like it.*

After therapy that day, Katrina informed me a doctor was
scheduled to plug my trachea. "This is exciting, Kate. No more
trachea tube and no more breathing treatments," she said. I was
scared and excited at the same time. The breathing treatments were
not going to be missed. Every four hours, a respiratory therapist had
been coming to my room. For twenty minutes I would sit with a
mask on over my face breathing in short quick breaths keeping my
lungs clear.

I remember when the doctor came to my room to perform the
procedure. I was scared, very scared.

The doctor calmed me down. "It's okay, Kate. You are getting
better. You'll be fine," she said. The procedure was quick and
painless. I was left with a red plug in my trachea. I looked in the
mirror. *The white bandage around my neck with this red plastic
plug looks like I'm wearing a bow tie.*

This time, I didn't cry. Somehow I had kept my sense of
humor. It was wonderful not having this tube dragging from my
neck. I had practiced my breathing and coughing on my own. I had
been worried that having the trachea tube removed meant I

wouldn't be able to breathe. The thought of suffocation was terrifying. The procedure worked. I no longer had to cover the tube to take a shower.

Over the next few weeks, my routine got easier. Dressing became easier, and Katrina assisted me when needed. I felt clumsy attempting to dress, but I didn't give up. I had progressed to standing and side-stepping into the shower. I remember the process of side-stepping over the ledge. This was a small ledge to step over, yet it was so hard for me. One small step for man, one huge leap for Kate. I was now wearing an air splint brace to give my leg support. Before wheeling me into the bathroom, Katrina put the brace and shoes on me.

"I want to make sure we protect your ankle," she said. *This sure is a lot of work for a shower.* I wheeled my chair to the edge of the ledge. "Okay Kate, come to a stance and reach with your arm for the grab bar," she instructed.

I leaned forward, getting out of my chair and facing the wall. I grabbed the bar and waited for her instruction. Katrina secured a gait belt around my waist. (A gait belt is a belt used by medical personnel to catch or hold on to the patient in shaky situations to prevent falls. It is usually made out of cotton or nylon.)

"Now, as you move into the shower stall, you will be shifting your weight back and forth on each leg. Follow along with my instructions and take it slowly. I'm going to stabilize your knee so it doesn't buckle," she said.

I listened to her suggestions. "Stepping over this ledge is going to be the biggest challenge for you. Go ahead and lift your right foot, remembering your weight should be on your left side. Steady now. Try not to be impulsive." Katrina assisted lifting my left foot over the ledge, as I gradually eased myself down, reaching for the shower chair.

"Good job Kate. The team has talked about a fitted brace being made for your foot. The brace will help to give more stability to the ankle," she said. *Wow! I made it this far. That was exhausting, I didn't realize how hard it would be.*

A weird looking device was made for my hand. The dome splint fit over my left knee with a piece of Dycem on the top. My hand lay on top, as I tried to activate the muscles in the arm. *Thank goodness I only have to wear this in the hospital! I wouldn't be seen in public wearing this.*

I got to watch the splint being made. The powder-like substance was heated in a frying pan, allowing the therapist to mold the material, which then created an instant hard surface.

Each day was an adventure into the unknown. Some days nothing happened and other days, a muscle that had been flaccid would suddenly twitch into life. Each time small miracles happened, it gave me hope.

From the Other Side of the Bed

I was committed to Kate's dream of walking out of the hospital. It was her dream – and it was mine. Kate gave it her best, but it was not to be.

Because I was so committed to her walking, I was at first resistant to learn about how to care for a paraplegic. To tell the truth, I was also hesitant because I am a klutz. I was afraid I would hurt Kate while moving her from the bed to the wheelchair. I had no choice. I had to learn to do it.

The first thing I was taught was how to transfer her from the bed to her wheelchair, then how to help her get on the commode. I was very unsure of myself. The very idea scared me.

One night, shortly after my lesson in transfer technique, I was faced with a medical emergency. Kate had to go to the bathroom and she could not hold it. I tried my best to get a nurse, but to no avail. It was all up to me. I grabbed Kate, (almost killing her) and plopped her on the commode. I was proud of myself when I got her where she needed to be.

Sadly. I forgot to take down her panties, so all I accomplished was to give her a comfortable seat on which to wet herself. At that point, we both started laughing so hard that I almost soiled myself.

Chapter Nine

~

Speaking of Eating

*I*t was wonderful to walk, see and hear, but nothing could match the joy I began to feel once I could communicate, especially with my children. The first tentative, primitive steps in communication had begun in ICU, where I had been given simple mouth exercises. These taught me to attempt to make strange sounds through my *Passy-Muir* valve. No one would make any promises that I would ever speak again (now they can't shut me up).

Steven continually encouraged me, telling me repeatedly and confidently that I would fully recover. He knew how much I loved flowers. While I was in rehab, he had fresh flowers delivered every Friday. I never knew if they meant I was getting better or if this was the week I would be having my funeral!

At Freeman Hospital I had a special, caring woman who helped me learn to reach out and touch the outside world with my own ideas and words. Norma was a tall, slender woman. She was a speech pathologist who became one of my best friends. Amy had been right; I would bond with a few special people. Besides Steven and Dr. Kolodney, Norma was my most devoted fan. She expected me to get better and her faith was contagious. Her expectation became my expectation.

Norma was worked into my regular schedule. She spent an hour or so with me every day. It was her job to teach me not only to speak, but also to swallow. I remember sitting in my wheelchair and Norma handing me a pen and paper, asking me to write my name. *Sure, this is no problem.* To my surprise, my name looked like chicken scratch! I was devastated. Norma reassured me that with practice it would get better. Her attitude of taking everything in stride was infectious.

Her good nature put me at ease. Whatever homework she left with me, Steven would see to it that I did it, again and again. They were a powerful team. Once again, he made a large sign instructing the nurses on how to use my speech valve.

Despite the sign, on one occasion the valve was not properly shut off. I was suffocating! I could not speak, much less call for help. I was about to pass out when he discovered me and started screaming for help. If he had not been around, I would have suffocated. Don't ever underestimate the power and value of visitors – not just for emotional support, but also for practical reasons. I was thankful there were non-medical people around me at all times.

Liquids were actually harder to safely swallow than solid food. Norma prepared my liquid diet with a special powdered solution called "thick-it" which made thin liquids lumpy and easier to swallow. I had an awfully hard time learning to swallow again. There was some fear that I would never again be able to drink liquids on my own. Norma stayed positive and kept me working on it.

After a few weeks, a very important day arrived. I was going to get a special test to see if I could swallow on my own. I would be seated in front of an x-ray machine and photographed as I swallowed liquids of various viscosities.

An energetic technician came bouncing into my room early one afternoon with a cheery "Hello Beautiful!" He transferred me onto a gurney and raised it so I was at a slight angle. *I'm nervous. This is the big moment. Please don't let me fail.* He wheeled me down to speech pathology. "I'll be back to wheel you upstairs after the test."

Norma patted my arm and comforted me with her soft voice, "Kate we have practiced for this day and I know you are ready. If you pass this test, you'll be able to start eating solid foods and we can get rid of the feeding tube." *I want so much to pass this.* "Let me sit you up a little more and place a pillow behind your back. Comfortable?" she asked. I nodded my head. *What's going to happen here? I'm nervous. I hate not knowing what to expect.*

"This is a relatively easy test, and there's no pain. It's very quick and involves taking some pictures and swallowing," she said. Norma explained the procedure to Steven, motioning him over to a small room with a window. I could see him standing behind the tinted glass with his arms folded. He had a look of trepidation. *I'm scared.*

"Okay Kate, let me show you what I've prepared," Norma said. "This is pureed applesauce mixed with a thick gooey paste substance called Barium. It's totally harmless (she forgot to mention that it was also totally disgusting) and shows us what's happening on the x-ray. We like to start with this so you won't aspirate." *What is aspirating?* Luckily for me, Steven asked Norma. "Aspirating is when you do not swallow food properly and it goes down the wrong pipe into your lungs," she explained as she scooped a small amount of Barium from the paper cup.

"I want you to take a portion of this and hold it in your mouth until I tell you to swallow," Norma said. She cautioned me to go slowly. "Okay, here we go. Ready?" she asked. I opened my mouth to take the applesauce, and held it in my mouth while Norma ran back to the screen. I panicked. *Hurry up. This won't stay in my mouth. I'm going to swallow it.* This seemed like an eternity.

"You can swallow now," she called. I was able to tolerate the pureed applesauce, coughing only slightly as it slid down my throat. "Good job Kate, we can now move onto the next item," she said. Steven could see the whole thing on the screen. He saw the food enter my mouth, my esophagus open and watched it go into my stomach.

Norma now filled a teaspoon of liquid from a paper cup. "I want you to swallow a little of this, but wait until I give you the cue," she reminded me. "Here we go, ready?" I held the liquid in my mouth while Norma ran back to the screen. *Hurry! I need to swallow.* "Now Kate!" she commanded. I swallowed on cue, immediately aspirating. I started coughing, my whole body shaking violently.

Steven came running. "Kate, are you okay? I could see it shoot right into your lungs!" Norma followed closely behind. I did not truly understand the real danger, but Norma and Steven did. I had just courted pneumonia, the number one killer of people in my condition.

Steven could not believe what he had seen. He had no idea if I could breathe or if I would get pneumonia or what. From the exam room, I was wheeled to x-ray, where I spent about an hour. Finally I was brought out to the hall with Norma beside me.

Norma summarized the results of the test, "Kate did fine with the thick liquid, but the thin liquid slipped straight into her lungs. We proved she can eat certain kinds of foods because she does have a primitive swallow reflex. I'm going to recommend she be put on a diet of pureed food." *Pureed foods? I haven't eaten for weeks and all I'm getting is baby food?* "We will try this test again later, but for now I recommend a diet of pureed food, which will at least allow her to begin tasting things again," she said.

From the Other Side of the Bed

I *was scared to death. I did not know how much damage had been done when she aspirated. I just kept praying that everything would be alright. To come so far and be felled by one stupid drink of water would be just too much. I was thankful when Kate finally came out of x-ray and I was told that she would be okay.*

Despite her amazing progress, things were much worse than Kate knew. She had no ability whatsoever to protect her air passage from liquids. The test was actually an abysmal failure. It was so bad that they actually thought Kate would never be able to eat normal food again.

Having all my foods pureed would be safe and allow me to be fed through the G-tube at night. Eventually I would have the G-tube removed permanently. I didn't realize at the time, but some people in my situation never swallow again.

"Absolutely no thin liquids for Kate," Norma told Steven "She will drown."

He looked at her curiously, "How long will it be before she can eat regular food?" *Yeah, that's what I want.* "Kate hasn't eaten for weeks. Can't we let her have something?" he pleaded.

"We need to stay with the pureed food and in a week or two we'll do another evaluation," Norma replied hopefully. "Maybe after that we can try thin liquids." Noticing I was teary-eyed, she patted my hand, "Oh Kate, you did great. I'm just being extra cautious." *I had hopes of eating something real. Now I can't even have a glass of water. I've failed.*

Norma again explained what happened to me. "Kate, liquids are going down the wrong way but you tolerate the applesauce okay because it is heavier than water. Let's hold off on any thin liquids for now."

"Let me illustrate it like this. If you take a cup of water and pour it on the floor, it moves really fast and breaks apart, not holding together. If you compare that with a cup of honey and do the same thing, it moves slowly staying together. You have weak muscles in your neck right now and the liquids are moving too fast for you to handle. That's why I want you to stay with everything pureed," she said. "I have to go now, but remember, you did fine."

The technician came to wheel the gurney upstairs. "Well, how did it go?" he asked cheerfully. "Not as well as we hoped," Steven said. "Oh you'll pass with flying colors next time. Very few patients pass the evaluations the first time," he reassured me. *I feel embarrassed failing this test. Everyone in rehab will want to know how I did.*

Norma instructed Steven to make sure a family member was present at meal times. At lunch Norma would sit in my room helping me to eat, and showing my family what to do. She encouraged me to sit in the wheelchair while I ate because that made it easier to digest the food.

A white hospital towel was draped around my neck and I was slowly spoon-fed the pureed food. Before long I started feeding myself. Often I missed my mouth, with the pureed food landing on my cheek. It was frustrating, lifting my quivering hand holding the teaspoon to my mouth. "Don't worry, that's why we have the towel, so take your time," Norma cautioned. *This is frustrating. This is embarrassing!*

"Slow down Katie babes," Mum reminded me. *I have no choice.*

Norma sat with me for about a week observing me and then suggested that I might enjoy entering an eating program. I could sit with others who had the same swallowing problems. Everyone was excited to have me join the eating group, except me. *I just want to go home.*

Norma could feel my discomfort. "Kate, you'll meet others with swallowing problems and it will get you out of this room," she expressed. *I don't want to leave this room.* "I don't feel comfortable leaving you by yourself," she added. "A therapist will be there to observe the group. I'll leave directions for the nurses, in case I'm not around."

A note was taped to my closet door giving strict instructions about swallowing. The sign read: "Kate is to take only small, bite-size portions, finish each bite, and put her fork down in between each bite. All liquids should be thickened – no straws!"

My food trays never looked appetizing. They consisted mainly of pureed turkey, mashed potatoes with gravy and pureed carrots. *This is disgusting!* About the only part I liked was vanilla custard or chocolate pudding. I always requested two of those.

Steven could not believe I could eat this food, nor could I; yet I ate every ounce I was given. *I need to eat to get better. No matter how bad this looks or tastes, I have to force myself to eat.* Nothing was easy or fun, including eating. It was a major ordeal. It was humiliating for me to have others watch me while I learned to eat again.

Mum continuously tried to sound encouraging, "You are a fragile wee thing. You need the energy. Come on, eat up." She helped prepare my tray by taking the Saran wrap off the containers. "Looks yummy, even pureed turkey on your plate." *I know I have to eat this stuff if I want to improve.*

It wasn't long before Norma gave me permission to start using a straw to take small sips of liquid. I could get juice from the rehab dining room during the day. I couldn't get enough of that delicious Kerns nectar-base juice; passion fruit, banana, kiwi, I loved it all, still do. "You are the first patient that I have ever let use a straw this early. I trust you and think you are ready," she said.

Gradually, I was upgraded to a soft mechanical diet and before the end of my discharge I was allowed to eat solid foods, with caution.

Every morning I started my day off with a delicious piece of cheesecake that Steven brought me. He was amazing. It seemed like there was nothing too small or too big that he wouldn't do for me. Steven had given up everything to care for me.

On Tuesdays, the team met with the neurologist, Dr. Alexander, discussing each patient's progress and goals for the following week. Amy discussed those with me and I looked forward to hearing what they were, because it gave me something to work toward. *Baby steps, just keep taking baby steps.*

I didn't know what to expect when I attended my first family conference with the team. My family wheeled me into the room where the team members and my doctor were seated in a circle. I was nervous. *This feels weird sitting in here and hearing everyone talk about me.*

Each team member gave a brief evaluation of my recovery. Dr. Alexander was pleased with my progress. Katrina reported that she had been working on the activities of daily living. "I'd like Kate to incorporate her left arm more into her activities," she said. (Even today, I must sit on the edge of the bed to dress. Standing while I dress is not an option.)

Delia shared how pleased she was with my progress. "Kate is a great patient to work with and willing to do the therapy," she said. *What choice do I have?*

No matter how kind and encouraging they were, some days I just hated it all.

Steven asked, "Well, what about Kate's left arm and leg? Are they going to come back?"

Delia took a deep breath, "We certainly hope so, but I can't say for certain. Sometimes we have to trick the muscles into working and we are doing everything we can to facilitate what does come back. As she improves, hopefully, we can use less and less equipment." *I hope so. Please let me walk again and use my arm.*

Joyce addressed some areas of concern. "We have put water back into Kate's diet during the day so she is not thirsty at night. There is a risk of pneumonia because of immobility," Joyce said.

"Is that something we need to be concerned with?" Mum asked.

"No, because now that she is moving and coughing more the risk is decreased. That is a common problem," she said.

"What about these leg spasms?" Mum asked. *Yes! I hate those. They always startle me.*

"I think over time that will get better. If we give Kate drugs for that, it will slow her recovery," Joyce explained, "and I don't think she wants that."

"Kate is doing really well and is very cooperative. She no longer needs cues about her swallowing and is able to use a straw. Liquids are very important," Norma said.

"When can she have thin liquids?" Steven asked.

"I'd like to keep her on thick liquids for a while. When her coughing and throat clearing is not a problem, then maybe we can try thin liquids," she replied.

The case manager, Desiree, finished out the session discussing her role with the insurance company. "I'm speaking with the external case manager on a weekly basis regarding her progress, goals and length of stay," she said.

"I don't want Kate leaving until she is medically ready to be discharged," Steven said. *What? Are you crazy? You don't have to live in this place. I want to go home.*

"There will come a point when her progress will slow down and the question will be, is twenty-four hour care needed and would Kate's needs be better met at home? These are questions we can address in our next family conference," Desiree said.

From the Other Side of the Bed

In this divided world of doctors, nurses, insurance companies and lawyers, it became clear that the people who wanted to help Kate the most were sometimes working for people who were interested more in saving money than saving lives.

The insurance companies' primary concern isn't the patient, it is the stockholder. They all are looking to save money and that sets up the battlefield. When your loved one's life or quality of life is at stake, you are not looking to save money. You want the best and the most, while the insurance companies are satisfied with good enough.

The people you need on your side, the case manager and team who meets with you at your family meetings, are under a lot of pressure. The case manager has to get along with the insurance company, on the one hand, and try to help you at the same time. Their job depends on how well they can balance these interests.

Some case managers are more patient-oriented and caring than others. They all have their own personal and professional skills, and remember, their ultimate boss is the hospital.

The care you get is limited to the money they can get for you, no more, unless you are willing and know how to fight.

There is an inside joke in these facilities about the HMO director who goes to heaven only to be told he can only have an over night stay.

One of the worst conditions that can face a patient is shortness of cash. Shortness of cash can kill.

Don't rely solely on the hospital staff to get your loved one the necessary care and treatment. You have to be proactive. You have to push. You have to risk being unpopular.

At your weekly team meetings, you must find out how long the insurance company has authorized for your loved one to stay in the hospital. They will reevaluate the hospital stay on an ongoing basis. At first, you might get authorization for a week at a time, and then maybe only days at a time.

Find out what treatment has been authorized and find out when the next reevaluation will occur. Get the team to explain to you what landmarks and goals the insurance company looks for when they determine how much more treatment will be allowed.

Once you understand what the insurance company is looking for, it is up to you to help see to it that the goals are met. You need to push when you see something that will help your case. Make sure it gets recorded in the medical charts.

Be pushy but nice. It is a tough balance. You can't offend everyone, but you must be vigilant. You cannot count on things getting written down unless you make sure it is done. Remember it is the squeaky wheel that gets the grease.

"Freeman Hospital doesn't have a contract for outpatient therapy so you may have to choose another facility," Desiree said. *What is she talking about?* I sat in my wheelchair listening to everyone, feeling more depressed and fighting back tears. *I don't want to be stuck in this wheelchair!*

The time came for Mum to go home to New Zealand. I knew I was going to dread this moment and really miss her. "I'm sorry but I have to get back, Katie babes. You are in good hands now," she said.

Mum, I don't want you to leave. Please don't go. I started crying. She put her arms around me, "I don't want to leave you, Honey, but I have to. You know how much I love you. My plane leaves this evening and I need to pack. I'll call you before leaving the airport." As she walked out of the room I started sobbing uncontrollably.

"Bye," she said wiping her tears with a tissue. *Damn! I can't stop crying. I am used to having her around. I wasn't planning on getting this upset.*

Steven called Mum from my room just before she had to leave for the airport. My ability to speak had slowly improved by then, so Steven held the phone to my ear to see if I could at least say goodbye, but I couldn't get anything intelligible to come out.

All I could do was sob into the mouthpiece. *Don't leave me, Mum.* "Kate, I have to leave, Honey. Are you there?"

Sobbing, I gasped for air. Mum finally hung up the phone. *Why did you put me through that Steven? I couldn't say a thing to her.* I spent the evening feeling depressed. *I don't want to see anyone. When will I see Mum again?*

"I will hear your sobs until my dying day. How I got on that plane, I'll never know," Mum told me in a later phone call. I didn't see her again for many years.

Chapter Ten

~

Moving On

$\mathcal{M}$eeting recreational therapists seemed a huge waste of time to me. *Recreational therapy? What's that? Why do I need recreation therapists?*

"My role is to get you to do some of the activities you did prior to your stroke," Caroline said when she was introduced to me. *Activities I did prior to the stroke? I was an exercise freak. How am I ever supposed to do anything like that again?* I was resistant to the idea of working with her.

"What kind of activities did Kate like?" Caroline asked Steven (remember, I was only able to speak a word or two faintly on occasion and then only with difficulty, so they still communicated a lot through Steven).

Things I'm certainly not going to be able to do now. My life will never be the same! I tried to hold back my tears. Listening to her reminded me of my past healthy life style and was depressing.

"Kate was very active before this," Steven said. "Hopefully we can replace some of those activities with something she can do," Caroline said. *I just want to walk – out of here.* She discussed my options while at Freeman Hospital. She talked about community outings, going to movies and restaurants and incorporating car transfers.

The first time I met Larry, another recreational therapist, he really aggravated me. He came into my room after visiting a much older patient in the next room. Speaking extremely slowly, but so loud he could have raised the dead, he said, "How - are - you? My name - is - Larry - and I'm a - re-cre-atio-nal therapist." *Yes, Larry, and I'm Kate and I'm not deaf.*

Larry visited patients in the early evening, encouraging us to get up and see the magic show, which took place in the dining room every Tuesday night. I came up with a nickname for him. *Oh, great, here comes Loud Larry and his traveling magic show! I'm too tired for this. I would consider going if a magic wand was waved over him and he'd disappear.* I never did go, mainly because I was exhausted from a day of therapy. I just didn't have the energy.

When Caroline wheeled me into the chapel for the first time, I broke down sobbing. *I don't care about a service. What's the point?* Caroline slowly wheeled my chair toward the altar. I sat there sobbing with a mixture of emotions that would have confused Sigmund Freud himself. "It's okay Kate, this is a natural response," she said touching my shoulder. *Just get me out of here!* I waved my arm toward the door. I wailed like a lost child as she wheeled me out of the chapel. *I don't want to ever go back there!*

Holidays are the loneliest times in a hospital. I will always remember Labor Day holiday weekend that year. The staff tried to have some kind of celebration to gather the patients together. The area was decorated and there was a barbeque for us. *I would rather be outside with my girls.* Loud Larry and Caroline had organized some activities for us, including one that was for our hand-coordination skills. *We can't even have fun without it being therapy.*

A blown-up paper target was pasted on the wall. We lined up behind each other in our wheelchairs waiting for our turn. *We look like we're lining up for a derby. This is dumb! Aiming with a water gun to squirt that? This sure looks like Loud Larry's doing.* As easy as it sounded, patients struggled to hit the target. I was next in line.

"Okay Kate," Larry said boisterously, dissolving my last ounce of patience and humanity, "just aim and shoot!"

Oh yeah, I'll aim and shoot, all right. I held the water gun up but instead of shooting at Larry's target, I turned and aimed right at him – and creamed him! Chuckling sinisterly to myself, I pulled the trigger faster and faster, totally drenching him. Loud Larry no longer talked slowly or clearly!

"Yikes! Help! No fair," he exclaimed. He held his hands up laughing and unsuccessfully trying to protect himself from my deadly aim. "Well, your motor skills sure are improving!" At least this brought a smile to my face. Loud Larry started to grow on me.

I spent the remainder of the afternoon with my family. It was just too depressing to listen to the other patients complain about what they couldn't do. Lying in bed that night I cried. *I hate being disabled.*

For most of my therapy sessions, Steven wheeled me to the gym so I didn't have to wait for a therapist. *I hate waiting. Besides this saves time.* As my strength increased, I wheeled myself to the gym using my one good leg, moving slowly but independently down the hall towards therapy, and eventual freedom.

Therapy was a process of baby steps and slowly I could see the miracles. Over time, I started insisting on doing exercises that felt more beneficial to me. There was a range-of-motion exercise where Delia had me lie down on the mat, placing one of my legs on a "powder board," allowing me to move my leg without much effort. The powder board was raised approximately seven inches above the floor. The therapist sprinkled talcum powder over the surface of the board (thus the name, powder board) to reduce friction, making it easier for me to move my leg back and forth.

Steven cheered me on, "Good job, Kate. Now keep trying." *You have no idea how hard this is.* I really had to concentrate on moving my leg. *Keep kneeling right in front of me, Steven. You are the perfect target.*

"Come on Kate. Really try to kick me. You can do it," he said. With every ounce of energy I moved my leg and to everyone's surprise my leg flew forward. *Oh my leg! It just moved.*

"Wow Kate," Steven said stumbling back doubled over in mock pain, then dramatically collapsing. He says he was pretending. I think I connected. *Let's try that again, Steven. That was fun.*

Everyone in the gym collapsed in laughter. *It felt good to laugh.*

Steven didn't care if I loved him or hated him. He just wanted me to walk again.

From the Other Side of the Bed

I pushed Kate; and then pushed her some more. I don't know if I was right or wrong to be so pushy. I did know that there was plenty of time to work out our relationship after Kate finished her therapy. I was Kate's coach and I don't know if anyone loves their coach or not. You hope they respect you, but at the same time you know that they may well resent you, sometimes even after they win the prize.

Kate had amazing focus. She did the hard work 24 hours a day and I did my jobm which was to spend every waking moment pushing her one step further than maybe she wanted to go.

She is right; at that time, it didn't matter to me if she loved me or hated me; I just wanted her to get well.

Chapter Eleven

~

To There and Back

*R*ehabilitation was hard work and a constant challenge. I was in agonizing pain at the end of each workout. My muscles were constantly sore.

I remember the morning Delia had me trying to walk with the aid of the parallel bars. "This is something we use to check your gait pattern," she said. *I've wanted to try these, but that was when I had two good hands.*

Delia set the brakes on my chair and stood behind me supporting my torso while Steven held my paralyzed hand firmly on the rail. Delia adjusted the bars so they were waist high for me. "Don't worry, Kate, I'm right here," she said. "Try to remember your hip control and gradually bring your foot through as you take a step." *She makes it sound so simple – it isn't!*

"We have you, Kate, you can do this," Steven said. Slowly I took a step forward with my right leg, trying to swing my other foot through.

That was awkward, like I'm lifting a dead weight. I looked down involuntarily thinking for a second that my left leg had turned into a log. It was the first time I realized how heavy a paralyzed limb is.

"Take it slow, Kate," Delia cautioned, "Let's try that again and really focus your concentration. We are right here with you." *I'm going as fast as I can.*

"Stand up tall as if you are being pulled by a string; hold your stomach in; squeeze your shoulder blades; breathe." Delia sounded like a drill sergeant. Slowly I moved along the mat. Beads of sweat began to trickle down my forehead. We hadn't gone far when Delia thought I might need to sit down. "Steven, bring her wheelchair in behind her, she is becoming fatigued."

He wheeled the chair onto the rubber mat and Delia supported me as I sat down. *Ahhh! That's a relief.*

My first attempt at using the parallel bars was pathetic. "I think we will do better at this exercise once Kate has her brace. It will give her the knee support she needs," Delia said.

With the decision the team had made for my brace, a cast of my leg was done for the fitting. "The brace will make it easier for you to walk, Kate. It will help with the foot drop and knee control." *Is this something I'll always have to wear? Can I wear this with shoes?* Delia noticed the fear in my eyes. "Don't worry. The ankle-foot brace is designed to fit inside your shoe. We are hoping this will be a temporary thing." (It wasn't temporary. I still wear it.) "In the meantime, we will continue to work on your walking in therapy."

I was nervous when Delia wheeled me to meet the orthopedist. I waited firmly seated in my wheelchair, brakes on. *I wonder how this is done.* "Hi, I'm Mike. So, we are going to fit you for a brace," he said. Mike began making preparations as I sat there watching him.

He had the hands of a worker, which reminded me of my father. A film of white dust covered his clothes. "Just sit there and relax," he said, spreading a white sheet on the floor. He crouched down and slipped a knee-high pantyhose on my leg. He used an ink pencil to mark the various spots on the panty hose. He ran a long thin piece of plastic down the center of my leg. *Wonder what that is for?* He worked in silence. *What the heck is he doing?*

He soaked the plaster bandages in tepid water and then gently wrung them out. Unrolling the bandages, he wrapped them evenly around my foot and leg up to my knee. Like a potter at the wheel, his hands caressed the plaster, smoothing it out. He had a rhythm as he worked; his hands covered with the thick, gooey, white mixture. Slowly the plaster hardened, and again he marked the cast with an ink pen. He ran a knife down the center to pry the cast open. *So that's why that plastic is there!*

Mike used some cast spreaders to gently ease my leg out. I was left with a thin white layer of plaster on my leg, which he carefully rubbed off. "I'll be back next week with your custom-made brace," he said.

"Thanks, Mike. We'll see you later," Delia said, as she released the brakes on my wheelchair. I thanked him with a smile.

When it came time to try my new brace, Delia eased my foot into place. The brace felt firm and weird. "This will help provide support. We will still work on strengthening your weak muscles," she said, "but this brace will keep your foot from rolling."

I stood up from my wheelchair and grasped the bar with my good hand.

"This will also help control your foot drop, and prevent your foot from dragging," Delia said, as I slowly took a step and tried bringing my left foot through. *I feel like I am dragging ten tons of led.* The brace (AFO) was made of plastic and came up to my knee. There was a buckle that a Velcro strap went through at the top.

From the Other Side of the Bed

One of my lowest moments was seeing Kate's first workout on the parallel bars. I was horrified by what I saw. I had so much faith, but after seeing Kate on the bars, I just could not see how this could possibly work out. Getting from where I saw her to actually walking just seemed impossible.

*I went home in despair that night shaken by what I
had seen. I prayed all night, and once again I somehow
came to a peaceful place. I realized that from my vantage
point, it did look impossible, but Kate wasn't giving up
and God wouldn't give up either, so....*

The process was slow. Results, although satisfying to others,
were not fast enough for me. I have had lots of miracles, most of
them small and almost unnoticed. I went from total paralysis to
where I was in only a few months. I had regained the use of my
right side, my double vision was dissipating and I was eating
pureed foods. Little by little my speech was coming back. I still
could not speak more than two or three words at a time and my left
side was mostly paralyzed, but I was alive.

Because of the emotional lability caused by the stroke, I was
on an emotional rollercoaster ride. I had a hard time understanding
why I could swing from delightful victory to fear and tears in a split
second. The mere fact that I has survived was a lot to be grateful
for, but I was impatient. I wanted to be how I used to be, and I
wanted it now!

It was Erma Bombeck who wrote, *If Life is a Bowl of
Cherries, What are we Doing in the Pits?*

Some days I felt great and could see my progress; other times
I was depressed because it wasn't happening fast enough. Getting
through therapy was a struggle. Learning how to tie tennis shoes
was impossible. *How can I do this with one hand?*

Prior to my stroke, I loved shoes. Ties and buckles or slip-ons,
I loved them all. Now, it was only sensible athletic shoes with long
thick laces.

"Kate, you need to learn to tie your own laces. Let me show
you the one handed way," Katrina would tell me. *There is no way
I'm going to learn that. I won't need to, because I'm going to get
the use of my arm.*

"No." I said, the one word that was so easy to say. I said it
emphatically, "NO!" I said again.

Each morning, as soon as I opened my eyes, I prayed that God would give me the strength to make it through the day.

I focused on Psalm 116:8, "I have delivered your life from death, your eyes from tears, and your feet from stumbling and falling. When you need relief, come to me in spirit and truth and you will find it."

I have never prayed so much in my life as I did during this time. "It's only for a season," Sister Delores would tell me as she taped up another scripture on my wall. My room was filled with scriptures that she posted each week. *Well, let the season be over soon.* Life is full of ups and downs, but I believe it is how we react to the adversity that molds our lives. I have been delivered from death; for that I'm grateful.

I'm reminded of the story about the teacup. The heat in the kiln was so intense that the cup screamed, "What are you doing to me?" The fire made the cup into a beautiful work of art that could stand the test of time. Just like the teacup, I was forced into the potter's oven of circumstances. I didn't feel like a hero or anyone special. I was afraid and I didn't want to be there; but I didn't have a choice, except maybe to give in and give up, and I wasn't about to do that, especially now.

The Bible teaches us that trials come to test our faith and produce in us the quality of endurance. I had to believe God was molding my life for a greater purpose. There was nothing I could do but stay in the oven until God decided I was done – not done for!

Chapter Twelve

~

Quarantine

*I*t was a beautiful August 14th. I could hardly wait for the picnic we had planned for later that afternoon. It was Steven's forty-eighth birthday. Our family had been through so much since that awful day of June 29th. We were ready for some celebration. I awoke that morning excited about the picnic in the park. I had my usual therapy session. After lunch I was advised I would not be receiving any more therapy today. *What is happening now? Why am I not having therapy?*

A sign was posted on my door. QUARANTINE: NO ONE IS TO ENTER WITHOUT SPECIAL PERMISSION. Nurses started wearing gowns, rubber gloves and masks around me.

What is going on? What could be wrong that I have been quarantined? Everyone around me seems frightened. Where is Steven? Where? I need him here to sort this out. I'm being totally ignored.

Like clockwork, Steven showed up every morning for my therapy sessions. He stayed until lunchtime, then left to return at three o'clock in the afternoon, bringing my daughters. Amanda usually took the girls directly to the park while Steven came to my room to get me. I looked forward to these daily visits. He was excited about celebrating his birthday with me, but when he arrived to wheel me to the park, he was dismayed to see the quarantine sign.

On the verge of hysteria, he ran to the nurses' station. This newest problem was just too much for him. He had the doctor paged to find out why I was quarantined. When Steven returned to my room he was wearing a gown, mask and gloves. *What the heck is going on?* "What – is – happening?" I said, taking short breaths to force out each word.

"Kate, I'll get to the bottom of this," Steven said. *I feel like an outcast with everyone wearing this stuff around me. I hate this!*

"Don't be scared. We have been through so much together. I cannot imagine this being too serious," he said. *Who is he kidding? No big deal? The entire hospital has stamped "leprosy" all over my room! No big deal? What is wrong with me?* My positive attitude melted like an ice cube on a hot sidewalk in August.

Finally, Steven learned the reason for the quarantine. I had brought with me the infection I had suffered at Torrance Memorial Hospital. This kind of infection had never been at Freeman Hospital. Everyone was concerned it could spread throughout the hospital. After running a culture test it turned out that my feeding tube was growing the same deadly pseudomonas bacteria I had in ICU. The infection was resistant to all known antibodies. No one knew how to kill this bug or how far it could spread.

"I would feel more comfortable if the tube was removed. This is awful to put her through this," Steven said. Trying to put on a happy face, he remained calm but he was shaking with fear. *Some birthday party this is going to be for Steven!*

Steven demanded an infectious disease specialist be called, but the staff had beaten him to it. He questioned at length the infectious disease specialist, internist, lung specialist, and speech pathologist. Steven was convinced that I no longer needed the feeding tube. Confident that I could make it without it, he insisted it be removed immediately. The pros and cons were debated in an emergency staff meeting. The doctors wanted to be sure I could take in enough food on my own.

"Turn the tube off today and let's see how she does," Steven said. He felt the risk of having to feed me by IVs was not as high as having me die of a bacterial infection. The doctors were reluctant. They explained the surgical procedure for removing the tube, which was not as straightforward as Steven had hoped. He feared the procedure could spread the infection, and instead of an infected feeding tube, he would have an infected wife.

Nevertheless, he demanded that the feeding tube be turned off, and asked that I receive all nourishment from pureed foods. Steven wanted the deadly feeding tube removed the next day. Once again it was he against the medical establishment. Nothing was done that day.

Steven had a plan, which he did not let me in on, and I had no clue until it was over. Presenting himself bright and early the next day at the nurse's station, he informed the nurses that he wanted a surgeon called immediately. "I want this feeding tube removed now, right now," he firmly said. A red circle of infection was appearing around my belly button. He refused to wait a moment longer.

The nurses told Steven nothing could be done. They agreed to make a note in my chart. "Nonsense! You could get someone here in five minutes if you wanted to. I intend to stay here until a surgeon is called," he said. He stood waiting patiently, arms folded across his chest. "Mr. Klugman, we simply cannot call anyone from here. I'm sorry we can't help you," the head nurse said.

"I just want to save my wife's life. It's up to you people. Can't you help me?" he pleaded. No answer. Remembering that pleading wasn't his best skill, Steven switched to attorney mode, "Okay, hand me a phone book and I will call a doctor myself. I'll get someone here to perform the procedure."

"You cannot do that," the nurse said.

"Like hell I can't!" he yelled.

Luckily for Steven, the other nurse on duty that day was a substitute from the nurse's registry, and she supported his decision. "This man is trying to save his wife's life. Why aren't we helping him instead of fighting him?" She handed Steven the phone book.

Steven began thumbing through the yellow pages, randomly calling doctors. Letting out a sigh, the head nurse finally grabbed the phone book from Steven and placed a call. Within fifteen minutes a surgeon arrived prepared to perform the procedure.

Steven expressed his concern about the procedure spreading the deadly infection. "Oh don't worry about that," the doctor said. "What do you mean?" Steven asked.

"Pseudomonas can't live in the stomach. There is no chance the infection can spread. The stomach acids would kill it," he said.

"Good Lord! Well, why did they put us through this? I have been going through hell and now you tell me it was all for nothing?" Steven said.

"I don't know. Anyway, don't be alarmed. This will be over in less than an hour," the doctor said.

Steven came to my room to give me the news. I was taken by gurney downstairs. A nurse reassured me everything would be fine. *I hope you are right.* I felt the sharp prick of a needle as they injected the sedative. "You should start to feel groggy in a moment. When the pain medication starts working the doctor can begin," she said. She left the room and I was alone in silence with my thoughts. *I wish this was over. What am I going to feel?* Steven waited patiently outside.

Before long, a doctor came in. "Okay Kate, this will be over before you know it," he said, putting gloves on. *Just start. I want this thing out!*

The procedure was quick but the pain intense. *Oh God, I thought I wouldn't feel anything! I can't take this! I'm going to throw up. Something is being ripped up through my stomach. I can feel the tube being pulled! Is this coming out through my mouth?*

Just when I felt I couldn't stand the pain one more second, I heard the doctor. "Okay, it's out." *Thank God!*

I felt light-headed from shock. I lay exhausted on the gurney while I was wheeled back to my room.

"Good job, Kate. Now you have gotten rid of these tubes," Steven said, relieved. *You have no idea how intense that pain was.*

Somehow I lived through it. I glanced at the clock on the wall. It was 2:45 p.m. and I usually saw Delia for my 3 p.m. therapy session. "Tell Del-ia I -want - my - ther - a - py."

"But you just had surgery. I think you should rest," Steven insisted.

I told him I could do this. Besides I wasn't given that much pain medication. I could do some therapy from the bed. *The quicker I can get out of this place the better.*

"Go." I sent him off with a wave of my hand.

"You're not the only stubborn person in this place," he muttered leaving the room.

Sheepishly, he informed Delia of my desire to do therapy. "Yes, I figured Kate would want that. I have never seen anyone so determined."

"Stubborn and ornery is more like it," Steven muttered.

From the Other Side of the Bed

*O*f course, Kate is not the only one who is stubborn and ornery. I really was desperate. I could have been tackled by security for my behavior, but I did not care.

Kate is kind in her telling of the story. I was much worse. Not only did I demand a surgeon be paged. I refused to let anyone leave the nurses' station. I was determined to shut down the floor until I got my way. I half expected to be arrested, but I was going to get that tube removed!

It happens all the time with medical care. Kate's doctors were not talking to each other. When the surgeon finally showed up he told me I had no worries. Pseudomonas does not grow in the stomach. Stomach acids kill it. My tantrum was unnecessary; Kate was never in any danger.

Big victory or empty one, I did get that tube out.
Within twenty minutes of the time I barricaded the nurses'
station with my body, Kate was in surgery. To her amazing
credit when she got out of surgery, she insisted on keeping
her therapy appointment.
  Kate was relentless in her pursuit of a full recovery.
  I was relentless in my support of my wife.

"I have some exercises we can do with her from the bed,"
Delia said. She gave me some simple range of motion exercises
requiring little effort. *I will do anything to walk again! I can't miss*
therapy, even if I have to do it from my bed.

Dr. Jeffrey Saver's Comments

*S*troke patients are at elevated risk for a variety of medical
illnesses. Loss of control over swallowing increases the chance of
bacteria entering the lungs and causing pneumonia. Prolonged
bed rest fosters the formation of blood clots in leg veins and skin
breakdown. Tubes into the lungs, stomach, and bladder allow
bacteria to migrate past the skin and cause internal infections. In
the past, most stroke patients died from one or another of these
medical complications of stroke. Modern supportive care is
designed to reduce the risk of developing supervening medical
illness, but they remain a common cause of setback and distress
in the rehabilitation process.

Chapter Thirteen

~

Cooking on All Burners

*M*y therapists began including the cooking group as part of my therapy. I had finally met the criteria for being able to eat real food and began cooking classes on Wednesdays. My diet was soft food. Katrina's goal for me was to become self-sufficient in the kitchen. *I've never been self-sufficient in the kitchen, so why do I want to put myself through this agonizing process? How do I cook with one arm? Easy. The same way I always have. I use my one good arm to pick up the phone and order takeout.*

The first time I was wheeled to the apartment, I thought I was going to be alone in the kitchen. To my surprise there were six other patients. *How the heck are we all going to move about in this tiny kitchen?*

All of us were at different stages in our recovery. Two of us were in wheelchairs; some were using walkers and canes. Katrina briefly introduced me to everyone.

"Kate, you will be situated at the counter learning how to stand while you prepare food," she said.

I waited patiently in my wheelchair as Katrina organized each patient. *This is going to take forever.*

Katrina situated a couple of the patients who had trouble standing at the table. "The best part of this therapy is that everyone gets to sit down and eat the meal you have prepared." *I'm not sure I want to eat anything I've prepared!*

The task I was given was to make chocolate pudding for dessert. *This will be easy. There's nothing to chocolate pudding.*

Little did I know what awaited me, and the kitchen.

Katrina handed me the pudding box and waited with folded arms for me to open it. *I can do this!* I cleverly used my teeth to rip open the packet and "poof" powdery chocolate flew everywhere. What remained went into the bowl, and I adjusted the milk portion accordingly.

To speed the process, Katrina attached the beaters to a handheld mixer and turned it on for me. I began mixing. Suddenly, the beaters came loose, flinging lumpy globs of pudding all over the kitchen and everyone in it! *What a mess. Is this a cooking or cleaning class? Everything is therapy. My, how I've taken things for granted.* What normally took five minutes to prepare, now took me an hour.

"Don't forget your posture, Kate," she reminded. *Posture?*

The next challenge was to pour the pudding mixture into individual bowls. *An extra hand would help right now.* Katrina held the bowl at an angle as the mixture sluggishly poured into the bowls. She scooped out the remaining pudding and put it in the fridge to set. Making chocolate pudding became easier and less messy each week. Katrina would situate my wheelchair behind me so I could sit if standing became a problem. She gave me constant reminders on my posture. *I know, I know. Squeeze the shoulder blades. Hold my stomach in. Push weight through my arm.*

"Pretend you have a hundred dollar bill between your butt cheeks," Delia said laughing. *Yeah, then I would be motivated.*

After we cooked each meal, we sat down and ate it. Since my weight was down, eating chocolate pudding became my favorite pastime. In addition, Steven brought me cheesecake daily. Eventually, both had to stop because the dietician changed my eating plan to low fat.

Over lunch Katrina discussed with us what we were going to cook that next week. Diet plans were taken into consideration. She jotted down the ingredients and went grocery shopping the week prior to the class. "It has to be something healthy and include a job for everyone," she stressed. Those of us who could speak certainly voiced our opinions on what should be cooked.

Ultimately the final decision came from Katrina. I offered to make fresh fruit salad with strawberries and kiwi fruit. I became known as Kiwi Girl because I made this fruit salad every week. Everyone at the table would start laughing at my meal suggestion. "Oh no, Kate, not the fruit salad again," Katrina would say. *Making fruit salad with one arm isn't easy.* I haven't made a strawberry and kiwi fruit salad since.

Katrina helped me peel the kiwi fruit and I sliced them using the chopping board with a couple of stainless steel nails sticking up through the middle. The nails made it easier to steady whatever I was chopping. I washed strawberries, sliced them and put them in the bowl. The chopping board was great. It is often a topic of conversation today for anyone who comes into my kitchen, because it has allowed me some independence.

Weekly meals rotated between pasta, stir fry, and lasagna. Cooking was exhausting. Even preparing these simple meals is a huge task for anyone with physical limitations. All of us required naps after lunch. I became more sociable as my speech slowly improved.

New patients to the group often asked, "What happened to you?"

As I slowly explained what had happened, they were amazed. No one could believe I had suffered a stroke at such a young age.

During lunches, Katrina made it a point to go around the table and have each patient say their name and why they were in the hospital. This gave us the chance to get to know each other and also gave us an opportunity to practice speaking. Some patients took a long time to complete a sentence due to their speech problems. We sat patiently, letting each patient express themselves. I was improving fairly rapidly now and I fought back the urge to finish their sentences when they struggled for words.

The cooking group helped me realize that we all had different limitations, but one goal in common: to get better. Even though I had far to go, I was now the best speaker in the group. However, I was clearly the worst cook!

One afternoon while I was resting, Amy stopped by. I appreciated my time alone with her, and felt safe enough to tell her anything. "How was cooking today?" she asked. "Good - but - exhausting," I replied slowly. Amy listened patiently as I struggled to express my fears and concerns about the transition to home and being with my daughters again. "I - want - to feel - closer - to my - daughters."

"You will. It will take time," she said. "Maybe you could try a fun activity such as blowing bubbles with your daughters. The girls will feel their mom is doing something fun with them and besides, all kids love blowing bubbles." Amy was sneaky, blowing bubbles would also help me improve my breathing and speech.

"Great - idea. They love - bubbles," I said. "Also - I feel - better about - my wheelchair. It helps me - get around - and not be a - hindrance."

"For right now Kate, it's a necessity," Amy said. "You will be discharged from the hospital soon, and it's important for the team and your family to discuss your needs. The hospital allows you to stay in the apartment overnight prior to your discharge to see if there are any remaining issues to address. You are familiar with the kitchen now," Amy said. *Spending time in the kitchen has never been my thing.*

"I'll be - fine. I'm - not staying - in the apartment. I just want - to be home - in my own bed." *I don't want to stay in the apartment. I'm overwhelmed just learning to walk.*

"Well, okay Kate, you sound like you are ready to go home," Amy said.

"Yes - I'm looking - forward to it. There's - so much - I want to do - to get my house - in order," I said.

"Just remember, when you do go home, take it slow. It's going to be an adjustment," she said. She left me with that thought.

While wheeling myself around the hospital floors, I would often cross paths with Sister Delores in the hallway. Sister would spur me on, "You can do it Kate!" "Way to go!" "Far Out!" "Good job!" She always had a smile on her face matching her upbeat personality.

It would make me chuckle hearing the juvenile phrases come out of her dignified mouth. I had never met a nun like her. "Baby steps Kate," she'd remind me. *That's true, but it's not fast enough for me. I want to walk – now.* Sister Delores was always affirming and positive, believing I would have yet another miracle.

Joyce, the head nurse, grew on me. She encouraged me to yell her name out if I needed help rather than pushing the call button. "Don't push the button Kate, strengthen those muscles and yell for me," she told me. She was right. I needed to develop volume. I was no longer a quiet timid person. She constantly urged me to strive for independence. Until now, my answers to questions had been a simple yes or no. Speech was painfully slow and distorted. By practicing breathing and talking more, my sentences became longer and smoother.

Therapists could hardly keep up with my endless requests for information. "Did I do - okay? Will I - walk - again? How long - before I - walk?" *I have to know.*

"Kate, you have to work at it," I was repeatedly told. I was determined to get better. I asked Delia what kind of exercises I could do from the bed. "Well Kate," she said. "Try to practice bridging." *Bridging?* "Lift your butt up, squeezing your butt cheeks together, hips raised high. Hold it in that position for a count of ten, then repeat," she said.

This I could manage. It was an exercise I was familiar with, having had the bedpan slid under me so many times. The therapists hesitated to give me too many exercises. They could tell I was determined to get better but wanted me to relax. "Don't overdo it Kate, you need to rest," they'd say.

I had the same routine each day. At 7 a.m. an attendant came to my room to wake me. Helping me transfer into my wheelchair, he wrapped a blanket around my shoulders and wheeled me to the dining room. Part of my therapy was eating with six others around a circular table where we had breakfast and lunch. In the beginning, I found the group meals difficult, just like my cooking sessions. Towels were draped around our necks as bibs, then we had to wait patiently while our carefully prepared trays were placed in front of us. Independance was incouraged, I had to master opening a small carton of milk by prying it open with the prongs of a fork, using one hand.

I was the youngest stroke survivor in the group. Miriam Brown, a dear lady in her late 80s, always insisted on extra napkins as she ate. Miriam and I became close and continued our friendship when we were discharged from the hospital. She loved my daughters and treated them as though they were her own grandchildren.

Christmas day, 2000, Miriam passed away. We were unlikely partners, separated by two generations in age but joined by a common struggle. In fact, the entire group was made up of a cross cultural and economic mix of people who, under any normal experience, would never have crossed paths. We were kind of like survivors on a desert island.

There was Pedro, who spoke no English. Conversations with him were out, but his indomitable spirit was always welcome at the table.

We had a petite Asian woman whose daughter came every morning to assist her.

Pearl, in her 60s, was assisted by one of her sons. She was blinded by her stroke.

Paul, an attorney in his 40s, had been a runner prior to his stroke. Now, in a wheelchair, he managed to amuse the group with his dry sense of humor.

Mr. Parker, a retiree in his eighties, joined me in his dislike of being in the hospital. At night he could frequently be heard screaming from his room, "I want to go home." He had no problem with breath support or vocalizing!

Because of our swallowing problems, and the danger of choking or aspirating, a speech therapist watched over us carefully as we ate.

Chapter Fourteen

~

Back to Normal – Back to Nordstrom

$\mathcal{A}$nother team conference was arranged so my brother and sister could take back information to my parents in New Zealand. Lynn and Tony were present along with Steven and me when the therapists gave their reports. Amy busily took notes. Norma began, "I recommend two or three weeks of speech therapy. Kate's breath support has improved and she is better at speaking and vocalizing sentences. She remains on thick liquids, slowly incorporating regular solid foods into her diet."

Delia spoke next, "Kate's mobility has improved immensely since she was admitted. At the moment, she needs 25 percent assistance moving in and out of bed. We are going to begin family training. In terms of equipment, we are looking at keeping her present model of wheelchair and a quad cane, the one with four feet." *I'm fine with keeping this wheelchair but a cane with four feet?*

Steven was curious. "What exactly is the procedure for family training? I'd like Kate to remain here and get as much therapy as she can. Is that possible?" he asked. *Are you crazy? I am sick of this place!*

"She is eager to go home. The family training is designed to help you feel comfortable with the wheelchair transfers and getting

167

her in and out of the shower and helping her with other needs she may have," Delia answered.

Katrina gave her input, "Kate has improved since the beginning from needing cues to being able to sit on a bench and take her shower. She needs help standing, but dresses with minimal assistance. Her shoulder movement is good; however, predictability of arm return is not presently known." *What! I have to get the use of my arm back.*

Amy listed items that I would need in the home: grab-bars, handheld shower head, shower chair, non-skid rubber mat and bedside commode. *Bedside commode? Grab bars?*

The meeting ended with Larry saying, "Kate is currently doing sedentary activity in the pool once a week. She's showing good progress there. As part of her therapy one of our goals is to include a therapeutic community outing each week. We think Kate is ready and has enough endurance to go on an outing." The team agreed. *Where will I go looking like this?*

From the Other Side of the Bed

The way it worked was amazing. At one point Blue Cross had cut Kate off from therapy. They did that late one Friday afternoon without any notice. I offered to run down to the hospital and bring them eighteen thousand in cash to cover another week of treatment. The hospital refused. Not only did they want to charge me as a private patient over sixteen thousand dollars more than they were willing to charge Blue Cross, they wouldn't even take my money. In reality, they did not want to treat Kate as a private patient at any price.

Kate and I had talked about how we wanted to make this whole horrible experience count for something special. We decided that we would dedicate this entire ordeal to making it easier for other people who would someday face the same problems.

We let the nurse know that Kate would be willing to speak to any patient who wanted to talk with her. When she first was admitted Kate was clearly the patient in the worst condition. She could not speak, she could not eat and she could not walk, or for that matter, move any large muscle group.

Now, here she is doing this amazing rehabilitation program. She worked so hard. Kate was so focused and had such a wonderful attitude that she inspired everyone around her. The doctors, therapists and nurses could hardly believe what they were seeing.

After a short time, the nurses began bringing all the new patients to visit my wife. They told the other stroke survivors that if she could do it, so could they.

There was a famous movie star in the hospital with Kate. I won't name her because her privacy was so important to her. Kate inspired her and made all the difference in her attitude.

If you think this sounds like I am proud of my Kate, you are right.

In my next session with Amy, I discussed my concerns about the upcoming outing. "What if - I start - laughing - no control?" I asked.

"Don't worry, just enjoy the outing, the laughing is a result of the stroke. You can't help that, Kate," she said.

She asked me if I would enjoy an outing to a local restaurant. "How about lunch at the local Sizzler?" she asked. *What could possibly be therapeutic about that? I just want to go shopping.* "I want to - go to - Nordstrom."

Katrina laughed, "Okay, I'll see what I can arrange." I think she thought I was joking, but the team discussed the idea and came up with ways to incorporate therapy into shopping. It was arranged. I would be going to the mall.

Caroline and Larry drove us to the mall. Two paralyzed teenage boys from my cooking group acompanied us in the van. They were not stroke survivors, however, both had been in motorcycle accidents. They rode with us going to the mall as part of their therapy. *Why do they have to come? Guys don't like shopping.* Larry securely strapped each wheelchair. *This is an ordeal for a shopping trip.* We sat patiently as he pulled the straps taut. I tried not to feel like a spectacle, sitting in a van for handicapped people.

Caroline sat in the back explaining some of the goals. "Kate, you can work on your standing and may utilize a public restroom," she said. *I don't plan on using the bathrooms. Some window shopping will be fine.* Forty five minutes later, the van pulled out of the hospital parking lot. *Finally, we are leaving.*

Steven wanted to be there for my first outing. He followed the van in his car along with my brother and sister. This was the first time I had ridden in a vehicle since my stroke and I was surprised at how extremely nauseated I felt. *When are we going to get there?* Thirty minutes later, Larry pulled into the parking lot. I looked up, and to my dismay, saw we were outside the wrong department store. *Why are we here? Nordstrom is on the other end of the mall.*

"Caroline. Why - are we - parked - here?" I asked.

"Well, this is part of your therapy. If you want the goods you are going to have to wheel yourself through the mall to Nordstrom," she said. *Oh great! I knew she would make me work. How embarrassing. People are going to stare.*

People did stare. They still do. And I still go shopping. There are some things you just do no matter what. I pulled myself along with my good leg, happily looking at the shop windows and being glad to be alive and out of the hospital. Larry and the two boys went to the food court. I made a bee-line to Nordstrom.

"Do you want me to push you, Kate?" my sister asked. *That would be wonderful. I'm already exhausted.*

"She's fine, this is part of her therapy," Caroline said.

Wheeling past Victoria's Secret, I decided to go in. Caroline and the others followed. I wheeled around the store with difficulty. *Pushing this wheelchair on carpet is a nightmare!*

"I'll buy you anything you want," Steven said. That was sweet, but I found it difficult to maneuver the wheelchair between the display tables. *Why the heck are these tables like this? Don't these people understand this is tough for someone in a wheelchair?*

The display tables were beautifully arranged with flowing cloths draped over them. Stacks of neatly folded bras and panties lay on top of each table. *These tables look nice but I feel like I'm in a maze. This being my first time shopping in a wheelchair, I never saw it from this perspective.* As I wheeled past one of the display tables, my wheel caught an end of the display cloth. The cloth slowly started twisting in the wheel. Suddenly I felt something heavy dragging along with me.

"Kate hold on," Caroline said laughing.

"Stop Kate, stop," Steven yelled. *What?* Lingerie items fell to the floor and I turned red when I realized what happened. *Oh my! Well, if I didn't want to be noticed before, I will be now.*

An assistant came rushing over. "Don't worry. I'll fix this," she said.

"Sorry, I'm learning to drive this thing," I said laughing.

Steven apologized profusely, explaining that it was my first outing into the community. Lynn quickly wheeled me out of the store.

Lynn and Tony could be heard laughing as we headed toward Nordstrom. "That was classic," Tony said gleefully.

Entering the store, I hesitated. Mustering a smile, I headed for the makeup counter where a friend worked. She was shocked to see me in a wheelchair.

I felt embarrassed seeing someone I knew, but I loved the quick makeover she gave me. *Wow! I feel terrific! I'm never going to wash this off.*

"You look like a new woman," Caroline said. "I'm sure you are tired. We need to head back." *I feel like a new woman. I learned something today – I only need one hand to pull out a credit card and sign my name. I'll be fine.*

In order to save time, Caroline briskly pushed me through the mall. *Oh sure, now you want to push me!*

We met up with Larry and the boys. "Wow, Kate, you look different," Larry said.

Yes I feel good.

I left my family and returned to the hospital. Larry began the process of getting each of us in the van. *This has been great, but I wish I was going home with my family.* The outing had left us exhausted. The day ended with an early dinner and then to bed. Tomorrow was a new day and more therapy.

From the Other Side of the Bed

T he normal outing for patients was a trip to the Sizzler restaurant, but Kate captured the staff and two eighteen-year-old boys, both quadriplegics, and they went where she wanted to go. I cannot imagine that the boys wanted to spend their first day out at Nordstrom. Kate prevailed, so off to Nordstrom we went.

Being in the mall was like a tonic for Kate, but it was bitter sweet. Her favorite thing in life, next to working out, had been shopping, and her favorite thing to shop for had always been shoes.

Now here was Kate, in her element, but it was not likely that she would be buying shoes anytime soon. Kate still cannot wear anything to walk in, other than tennis shoes. You could see both the gleam in Kate's eyes and the sadness. It was heartbreaking to see her dismay and yet good to see that she had made it back and life would go on.

A couple of days later during my self-care session Katrina said, "We have scheduled a home evaluation outing as part of your therapy." *Delia and I need to visit your home to make sure it's a safe* environment for you. We will make sure you can function in your own home," she said. *Does this mean I'll be going home soon – to stay? I don't want to go home to visit.* I smiled and said, "Great."

As we pulled into my driveway, I felt a strange sense of apprehension. *I never thought I'd see this day.* I was never absolutely sure I would make it. I could feel my heart beating fast. Delia assembled my chair and wheeled me to the front door.

"Mommy, Mommy," Stephanie said, blasting through the doorway and throwing her arms around me. My world turned into a kaleidoscope of gleeful kids, a barking dog, and a happy husband. I wasn't prepared for kids and a dog. I thought they would be in school and I would have a chance to adjust for a minute before they got home. This simple homecoming was anything but simple!

"Are you coming home today?" Stephanie asked. "No, Honey, I'm only here - for a couple of - hours," I told her. Delia explained to her that the house needed to be safe and friendly for me.

"Oh, okay. Look Mommy, it is friendly. Jenny is glad to see you," Stephanie said dragging the dog by its collar. *Oh, Jenny girl, I miss you too.*

"I kept the girls home from school today because they wanted to see you," Steven said excitedly. *I love seeing the girls but I need to concentrate and they should be in school.* "Everyone was excited about your visit and Amanda has been up since 5 a.m. cleaning," he said. I glanced around. *Well, things look okay, at least downstairs. I can't believe I'm inside my house again. Feels like I've been on a long vacation.*

Delia and Katrina walked around my house making suggestions. My mood suddenly changed. My eyes searched around the living room spotting things that upset me. *This is cluttered! I never kept a house like this. My plants are dead and there are crayon marks everywhere. This doesn't feel like my home.* "These throw rugs will have to be put away so you don't trip," Katrina said. *I love my rugs on the floor. It's going to look so bare.* "That's not a problem. I can remove those," Amanda said. *Whose house is this anyway!*

"Okay Kate, let's have you stand and try walking with the walker," Delia said wrapping a gate belt around my waist. I leaned on the walker and headed clumsily toward my kitchen.

"Think about lifting your left foot Kate, instead of dragging it," Delia said. *I'm doing the best I can.* I fumbled trying to step up onto the tile floor. *This is only a three-inch step. I can't believe how hard this is!*

I stood still, catching my breath, gazing around my kitchen that was once so neat and tidy. Sheets of yellow legal paper were taped above my stove listing instructions and phone numbers. My counter tops were scattered with odd items. *Nothing is organized. This is her idea of cleaning? I hate this.*

"Kate, we need to stay focused on your walking," Delia said. *I know, but this is the first time I've been home and I want to see how everything looks. Oh, I wish I could fix everything how I had it. I can see how difficult adjusting to this is going to be.* I turned the walker, taking slow steps. *Oh my! Even Rachel is growing up before my eyes. She's sitting in a booster chair now?* The high chair that sat in the kitchen corner was replaced with a brightly colored booster seat. *I feel weak and overwhelmed right now. I need to focus on getting healthier before I tackle this problem.*

"We will also need to put a couple of wheelchair ramps in for her. The house is a relatively open space, but she'll still need those," Delia said. *But my beautiful hardwood floor! My house is being rearranged so I can move around in this wheelchair.*

"Before any patient is discharged, we have to visit their home. This is routine Kate," Delia said. Two portable ramps that only required a piece of nonskid material under each end were set up.

The therapists suggested that I only use the downstairs portion of my house. Katrina took a quick look around the rest of the house.

"I can turn the den into a bedroom for Kate and there's a small bathroom she can use," Steven said.

"I think that will work fine, although there's no reason why she can't sleep upstairs at night," Katrina said. *Yes. I don't want to be down here by myself. I want to sleep in my master bedroom.*

"I want to sleep upstairs," I said. "Steven can carry - me upstairs at – night."

"I have a bad back." Steven replied. *Forget about your back. I've just had a stroke.*

"What if I need help?" I asked.

"I'll get you a tiny bell to ring, and Amanda or I will help." *A bell? What if no one hears me? This will be scary not having nurses nearby. What does Amanda know? She's here for the kids.*

"We need to make sure her wheelchair can fit comfortably through this bathroom door," Delia said.

Katrina measured the doorway, "This will work, but it's tight." She turned to me, "Try wheeling your chair through."

The chair fit through the door but I had barely enough room to wheel up to the shower door.

"Okay. Next let's try a dry run on seeing how you will transfer into the shower. I need to measure where the grab bars will go," she explained. *Grab bars? I feel old. Well, it's better than sponge baths.*

Setting the brakes on the chair, Katrina helped me step over the tiny ledge. Standing in the shower, I held onto the window ledge to balance myself. Suddenly, I was joined by kids and a dog.

Katrina smiled at my discomfiture. "That's how it is with kids and dogs. You'll have to get used to that. You haven't been around and they obviously miss you."

She continued, "Remember Kate, you will have a shower bench in here to sit on." She measured where the grab bars would go.

Katrina and Delia finished taking measurements and we headed back to the hospital. I sat in silence thinking of how my life used to be. When I got back to my room, Joyce asked, "How was your home visit?"

Distressed, I answered, "Depressing. Nothing is how - I used to - keep it."

"Kate," she responded, "you'll be home soon and can have people help you organize. Right now, you have to focus your energy on getting better. There's no point becoming agitated." *I know she's right. There is nothing I can do.*

That evening Steven and I talked about my visit home. "Are you going to be okay coming home not quite 100 percent?" he inquired. *Not quite 100 percent? Are you saying I'm not going to walk out of here?* I hadn't looked at it like that. I didn't answer. Steven didn't press it. It should have been obvious. This was the first time it hit me as to why they were talking about ramps. They assumed I was going home in a wheelchair. I refused to accept that. *I thought I was walking out of here.*

Another home outing came on a Saturday afternoon. Once home, I rested on the couch watching everyone around me. The den was being rearranged for my arrival home. My neighbors Rocky and Doreen, came over and offered the use of a hospital bed that had been sitting in their living room.

"Dad just passed away last week and you are welcome to use it before we return it," Doreen said. *Call me squeamish; call me superstitious; I don't want to sleep in a dead man's bed!*

"Great, I'll take you up on that offer," Steven said. *Oh gee, thanks Steven.*

All three left to bring the bed over. I transferred into my wheelchair to go outside to watch. *I guess this will work. Besides someone would have died in those hospital beds I used in ICU and rehab.*

Steven and Rocky wheeled the bed down the street. It was quite a sight. It fit perfectly into the den where I was going to sleep. I spent the remainder of the afternoon resting before I returned to the hospital.

Dr. Jeffrey Saver's Comments

*S*trokes can affect emotions in numerous ways. Nearly half of all stroke patients experience a period of depression following their stroke. In part, depressed mood is a natural reaction to the sudden alteration in life circumstances stroke brings about. In addition, brain lesions can directly compromise the neurotransmitter systems that underlie mood, producing depression by altering the brain circuitry of emotion.

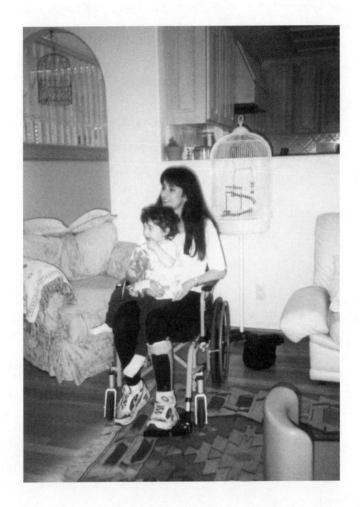

Kate back at home.

Chapter Fifteen

~

Homecoming

I had wonderful mental images of what it would be like to be home. Every spare moment had been spent dreaming about it, and now, I couldn't believe that day had finally arrived. Home had been a magical word; images of being with my daughters flashed through my mind. October 15, 1995, I was going home. I was ecstatic but apprehensive. *Is this really going to happen?*

My girlfriend Cherri arrived early Saturday morning to help me pack. Discharge was scheduled for 10 a.m.

"Where's Steven?" I asked.

"I don't know," she replied puzzled. *He knew I was coming home today. Where the heck is he?*

"Okay Kate, let's get started. We can do this without him. I don't have a lot of time," Cherri said. She had three or four cardboard boxes with her. I was astonished at all the things I had accumulated over the past few months. Sitting in my wheelchair, I watched Cherri pack my possessions. Diapers, bandages, diaper rash cream, a roll of toilet paper, a bottle of lotion, and a couple boxes of Kleenex were put in a box.

"I don't need those," I said in a determined voice.

Cherri replied, "You paid for those items, Kate, they are yours." Hesitating I asked, "Are you sure Cherri?" Laughing she

179

said, "They will be thrown away anyway." I don't really need the souvenirs, but at $50 a box, I guess I can keep the tissue.

Cherri loaded the two carts up, flowers and all. A nurse helped her wheel one of the carts down the hallway. I followed, pushing myself in the wheelchair with my strong leg. As we headed down the hallway, I saw Steven walking toward us.

"Oh, you've finished?" he asked in a surprised tone. *Great timing, Steven.*

Cherri was quick to answer, "Yes, but you can still help. Here, pull one of these carts."

Once downstairs in the parking lot, I watched as the boxes were put in the car. *At last I'm going home. I really am going home. This is it.*

Steven wheeled me around to the passenger side of the car. *I wonder if he remembers how to do a car transfer?* Katrina had given him lessons on wheelchair transfers. I felt more comfortable with Katrina transferring me. Steven managed without dropping me. *I can't say anything because I know he's doing his best.* We drove out of the hospital parking lot with few words being exchanged on the ride home. I was eager to get home.

That afternoon, Cherri helped me settle into my new surroundings.

The girls exploded into the room, excited I was home. "Mommy needs rest, girls. Don't bother her," Steven said.

Ignoring their dad, Stephanie and Rachel started bouncing on the bed. Stephanie holding the control panel started pushing the button to make the bed rise. Rachel shrieked, "Look at me Daddy!"

"Don't - let them - play - with that; it's - not - a toy," I said, rapidly getting dizzy. It was hard to get the words out and keep from throwing up at the same time.

"Stop it, Rachel. Stop it!" Steven said harshly. Both girls kept bouncing on the bed, neither listening. *So much for the peace I had dreamed of!* "They are glad to have their mom home," he said apologetically.

Cherri saved me. "Come on girls, get off there, I need to make the bed," she said walking into the room holding some sheets. The girls jumped off the bed and ran outside to play.

She helped me to a chair and made the bed with the new sheets she had purchased earlier that week. *I hate having to rely on people. I used to make my own bed.*

"Okay, I need to go. You get some rest," she said, kissing me on the cheek.

"Thanks for - helping," I said, trying not to resent my dependence.

Later that afternoon, we met some friends for dinner. It was a restaurant I especially liked. I had fantasized about eating there again; a fluffy baked potato and a succulent piece of charbroiled chicken. My mouth watered thinking about it. *I'm going to savor every bite.* I was ecstatic to be going. Our friends drove us to the restaurant early to avoid the crowds. Steven pushed my wheelchair up the sloping ramp, following the waitress. I could hear him muttering under his breath about how hard it was.

"Pull me up to the table. I'll transfer into the booth," I said.

"Are you sure?" he said.

"Yes, yes, I'm sure. Don't treat me like I'm disabled; I want to feel normal," I said, annoyed at the fact that I was, in fact, pretty severely disabled.

He helped me transfer, then folded my chair and placed it in the corner. The waitress handed us menus and took our drink order. "I'll be right back," she said smiling.

When she returned and began writing down the orders, my emotional lability kicked in and I started laughing – at nothing. *What is so darn funny?* I couldn't stop laughing to tell her what I wanted. *This is awful! What am I even laughing about?*

Steven simply said, "She has had a stroke and this is the first time she has been out for a meal with real food." *She's going to think I've been locked up for months. Well, I guess I have.*

The waitress smiled, "It's okay, take your time." The meal was marvelous, and I was grateful to be able to swallow each bite.

"I bet that tastes great, after eating hospital food," Rhonda said.

"No kidding," I replied. "I need to remember to take only small sips," I said lifting the glass to my lips. *Lord knows I don't need a coughing episode in here. I also don't want to have to use the bathroom.* Gone were the days when I could use a bathroom without much thought or planning. I dreaded having to use a bathroom in a public place, especially with the wheelchair.

We went to church that evening and I insisted that we enter after the service was in session. "I don't want people fawning over me," I told Steven. "It will be embarrassing if I start crying out of control, and I guarantee you I will."

As we proceeded into the room, a few heads turned, but the majority of the congregation continued to watch the pastor giving his sermon. Steven quietly pushed the wheelchair to a seat in the back of the room where we listened. Glancing up from his reading, the pastor noticed us sitting there, paused for a moment and took his glasses off, "I think we have a member who has something important to say."

Heads turned as he walked down the aisle holding a microphone. *No Zac, I hope you aren't walking this way. I just want to sit here. I'm not ready for this. Please don't make me say anything.*

Before I knew it, he was kneeling beside me. "Welcome back, Kate. Do you have anything you want to say?" he asked. *Anything I want to say?* Suddenly, I started crying uncontrollably. *I can't get any words out.*

"It's okay Kate, I'm sorry if I overwhelmed you," he said patting me on the shoulder.

The congregation rose to their feet applauding me. "We are all so proud of you," he said. I sat sobbing in my chair. *I wish they would stop clapping.* When the applause died down, the pastor went back to giving his sermon.

I felt stupid. *I hate this emotional lability. Why did I have to cry like that?* After the service, the congregation members came over to greet me. I felt overwhelmed with the sheer number of them. They were my friends and family, but living outside of the hospital was going to be tougher than I had imagined.

Nurses came to my house daily to assist me in getting showered and dressed. *There must be a way to do this myself. I hate having to rely on people. I feel like a broken doll that can't be fixed.* I could wheel my chair up to the edge of the shower door, but I needed help closing it. I could brush my hair before going to bed, but I could no longer braid it. I couldn't seem to do anything totally on my own. Everything seemed overwhelming.

The disarray in my house made me angry, depressed, and frustrated. *How could Steven have allowed this to happen? I want to get up out of this wheelchair and fix everything. I feel helpless. This mess isn't my home. This isn't me.*

I was frustrated with myself and disappointed with all the people around me. I was disappointed that I had not been able to walk into my home like I had planned. I was disappointed with the home care I was receiving. The therapists who came to my house to give me OT and PT were well meaning but, it was nothing like what I had become accustomed to receiving at Freeman Hospital. I was disappointed in everything.

In the next outpatient evaluation session that Steven and I attended, we were asked what I wanted to achieve. I told the therapists I wanted to be independent and walk again.

Steven made clear his unhappiness about the home therapy. He asked the case manager for some suggestions. She told him they had a wonderful outpatient program, but my insurance company would not cover it.

Steven would once again have to go toe-to-toe with the insurance company. Putting some kind of argument together, Steven got the company to agree to pay the outpatient therapy only if I agreed to waive home nursing help. It was complicated but it worked.

Thanks to the deal Steven worked out, I was able to continue outpatient therapy five days a week. Herlene, my new therapist, asked, "What are your goals, Kate?"

"I just want to get the use of my arm and hand back. You have to help," I said urgently.

"That is a goal of ours too. Is there anything else you want to accomplish while you are here?" she asked.

"I want to be able to hold my daughters," I told her.

"Well, let's see how we can attain that," she said.

During the weekly therapy sessions, Herlene practiced with me by improvising with two round balls in a pillowcase.

"Okay Kate, let's pretend this is your daughter and you are going to pick her up," Herlene said.

I started laughing. *Yeah, right!* "No laughing Kate, you have to concentrate," she said.

"But this is silly," I told her.

"Well, do you want to hold your daughters again?" Herlene asked. *Yes, you are right. I'm willing to try anything.* At first I struggled with one hand to grasp the balls through the pillowcase trying to imagine I was holding my squirming daughters.

At home, I practiced with the girls asking them to stand on the couch so I could lift them. The nanny stood by ready to catch them.

"Look, Nanny, Mom is holding me," Stephanie said. *Don't wriggle around too much Stephanie. I'm nervous. I need to stay steady.*

"Hold still, Stephanie."

"Good job, Mom."

"Okay girls, Mum has to rest," I told them. *It feels good reaching my goal of holding them.* Gradually, over the months I was able to comfortably hold them close, although I could not walk around with them. I had to stand in one spot. The girls loved taking turns being held. It was a good time. Reconnecting felt great.

That Thursday I had therapy and Steven insisted on going with me. *I really wish he wouldn't come today. I am not in a great mood.*

"I have an appointment with a new social worker," I told him.

"Oh good, I'd like to be there and meet her," he said. I told him I wanted to go by myself this first time, but he ignored me. He drove me to the hospital and wheeled me to the counselor's office. We were greeted with a warm smile.

"Hi, I'm Susan, please come in. You must be Kate. It's nice to meet you." After Steven introduced himself, she motioned him to a chair. I stayed in the wheelchair. "I've read over your file, it's quite a story," she said. "How does it feel being home?"

"It's still a challenge, but I believe we'll get through it," Steven responded. *I thought she was talking to me. Oh well.* My mind wandered as they spoke. *This is a waste of time. I'd rather have physical therapy. I wish I still had Amy as my social worker; I don't want a new one.* I had many feelings bottled up inside me.

"How are you feeling since you returned home Kate?" Susan asked me again.

"My house is in shambles," I said, frustrated. Turning to Steven I complained, "You should have seen that things were in order before I came home. How could you do that to me?"

Not waiting for Steven's response and perhaps giving him a chance to think of an answer, the social worker interjected, "I'm sure he did the best he could under the circumstances."

"I did everything I could, Kate," Steven said edgily. "Saving your life was more important than housekeeping." We argued back and forth. *I don't want to be here. They seem to be able to get along just fine without me.* Steven went on to explain to the social worker, "We have a nanny who had been our daughter's preschool teacher. She quit her job to come and take care of the girls. She seemed so stable, but I quickly found out she wasn't. I fired her."

I wondered why Steven was going on about this. This was not our marriage counselor, this was my therapy session. I was too tired to resist.

From the Other Side of the Bed

*O*ur nanny turned out to be mentally ill. She believed that she would be replacing Kate as my wife. She obtained a new driver license with my last name. She started *wearing my wife's clothes and began to fantasize about taking over for Kate. I know it sounds like a bad plot from a movie – The Hand That Rocks the Cradle II – but it happened.*

Since Amanda was spending so much time cooped up in the house, I had shown her how to use the internet.

The internet helped her take her fantasy one step further. Amanda found my credit card information and used it to order herself additional credit cards in her name and ended up spending a lot of money on herself with my credit.

After Kate was home for a few days she discovered credit card bills in the name of Amanda Klugman. Realizing what the housekeeper had been doing, Kate was horrified.

We called the police. Amanda was arrested and prosecuted. It was all such a nightmare. Now Kate not only was mad at me for letting the house get messy; she was mad at me for letting the Nanny run wild.

I listened to Steven go on and on. I didn't say anything. *Why are we talking about Amanda?*

Trying to control myself, I felt the feelings surface. Tears started to roll down my cheeks. *I knew this would happen. That's exactly why I didn't want him to come today. I have physical therapy soon. How am I supposed to concentrate?*

The counseling session turned into a nightmare with me crying uncontrollably. I couldn't even speak because I was so upset. I listened to Steven ramble on about his own issues while Susan listened and nodded supportively.

This is supposed to be a therapy session for me, not him. Now he has used up all my time. I'm the one who had the stroke. I was angry inside; mad with him, her, the world.

The hour dragged by and Susan finally announced the session had ended. *I feel worse, not better.*

"I'll see you next week, Kate. I'm sorry this was upsetting for you." *There won't be a next week!*

Steven wheeled me down the hallway as I sobbed into some tissue. My eyes were red and puffy. "How am I supposed to have physical therapy now," I cried waving my one good arm in the air. He walked behind me in silence, pushing my wheelchair. *I need to pull myself together. I can't let this interfere with my therapy. I have to concentrate.* I had a session to get through. I just couldn't focus.

Susan walked in during therapy and aked "Kate, can I see you next Thursday after your physical therapy?" *Oh no, you won't! I have no intentions of coming next Thursday.*

"She'll be there. Thank you Susan, for rearranging your schedule for us," Steven said.

Therapy didn't go well. The therapist suggested I go home and rest. *I hate missing physical therapy. I just can't focus being this upset. Damn those two!*

There was silence between us on the drive home. A couple of times, Steven tried bringing up the subject.

"I can't talk about this. I don't want to talk about it," I said firmly. *I know I'm going to start crying if he brings this up again.* We arrived at the house and he wheeled me inside.

I rolled down my ramp and into my room. I went to bed, refusing to speak to anyone. I was depressed and had a raging headache. I lay on my bed, my head spinning, wishing I hadn't let myself get that upset. *I'm not going back to that social worker, to heck with them all. I just don't care about the house, therapy, or anything!* I slept the remainder of the day.

Even though Steven was doing so much, I found myself each day feeling more and more resentful. I could not get over how badly he had managed the house and the nanny.

The next day I called the Women's Pastor and told her I wanted a divorce and to move back to New Zealand. She was stunned, but heard me out.

The following day the doorbell rang, and I found myself confronted by the Senior Pastor, his Associate Pastor, and the

Women's Pastor. *So much for trusting her!* They had come to help Steven and me save our marriage. I felt like I was on trial. Steven acted as if he had no idea this was coming. I told my story and Steven told his. The pastors asked questions and then came the verdict.

"Kate, it sounds like you are making a molehill into a mountain. We understand how you feel, but Steven has been a good man and a divorce isn't justified – besides, the church doesn't believe in divorce," Pastor Zac said.

Making a molehill into a mountain? How do you people know what I'm going through? The church, which had been so important to me, suddenly seemed against me.

From the Other Side of the Bed

*N*ow, the hour of our greatest discontent. "Home" had been a magic word – so powerful that it moved paralyzed limbs when medical science said it was impossible. Here we were home – but still, home was full of pain and loss.

Within a few days, my super hero aura was gone. I was no longer the man who saved her; I was the man who let the house get dirty.

Kate and I were seeing a therapist and he put it this way, "Mr. Klugman, your wife died in the hospital and a new woman was born. It is the new person, not your old wife, who has come home to live with you."

Each day the house reminded Kate of what she had lost and how she could no longer manage things. My former admittedly careless habits around the house were once cute, now they were irritating. I understand, after all, care-lessly discarded shoes in the middle of the living room, once a mild irritation, could now cause a serious fall.

I understood it in my head, but old habits are hard to break. Each day that I failed to pick up after myself, Kate had less and less good will toward me.

One morning the door bell rang. It was the Senior Pastor, the Associate Pastor and the Women's Pastor. I had no idea they would be showing up at our door, but there they were. Kate had apparently had a conversation with the pastor and she was worried. I think Kate had told her she wanted a divorce.

It felt like I was on trial. Kate was encouraged to speak her mind. According to her, I was lazy, messy, and thoughtless. At the end of the conversation, the pastor told Kate he thought she was making a molehill into a mountain.

I was sick at heart that it ended that way – that I am lazy. Maybe I was. I had put out so much energy in the hospital that I was exhausted. I had shut down.

Kate's demands seemed petty to me, I guess I did not give them the attention I should have. I wanted a medal. I was a hero, a legend in my own mind and I resented the lack of appreciation she seemed to demonstrate.

She asked me for a divorce, saying she was unhappy. I suggested that it was not my fault; that she was unhappy not because I had changed, but that she had changed. I was right. In a relationship, trying to prove you are right is the worst thing you can do.

I felt unappreciated, and Kate felt I was uncaring.

Steven had failed to take care of the house or manage the nanny. His habits drove me nuts. I always knew he was a slob. I did not mind so much when I was healthy, walking behind him cleaning up the path of destruction he left in his wake. Now I was physically unable to do anything to stem the raging tide of his messy habits. Besides it was now dangerous for me. I could break an ankle and I had no way of protecting myself if I fell. He didn't seem to understand – or care. My mind was made up. I wanted to take the girls and go to New Zealand.

I was scheduled to meet with Susan the following Thursday. I cancelled.

"Kate, please go. I won't come with you this time," Steven said.

"No, I'm not going. I don't like her as much as Amy," I said. I stayed in bed, cancelling physical therapy.

That night, Steven insisted I go out to dinner with him. During dinner I told him again that I wanted a divorce. He said, "No."

"I deserve to be happy, especially after my ordeal. I've paid such a high price to stay alive and I'm entitled to be happy. You are annoying, pushy, and on top of that, a slob," I said.

He replied, "Kate, you are not unhappy because of me but because of the stroke. I will not help you in any way if you wish to proceed with a divorce." He gave me a lecture on the sanctity of marriage. *I don't want to hear that, what I want is to be away from you.* The dinner produced a truce. I was very attached to the idea of ultimately getting away from him.

Susan called during the next morning and I chatted briefly with her. We decided I would go to the appointment next week without Steven. It made sense, because after all the sessions were for my benefit. *I'm the one who had a stroke.* Over the months I learned to trust Susan, expressing myself openly to her. I began to look forward to my sessions, finding her compassionate and caring.

I tried to work out my feelings about Steven, but I was still unhappy with our relationship. I had my life back, I felt out of control with the quality of it. Steven wasn't helping. The traits that made him my hero became the very traits that irritated me.

Sitting at my kitchen table one afternoon, I heard the doorbell. *I wonder who that is. It's like Grand Central Station around here.* I wheeled toward the front door. "Just a minute," I called as I pushed myself up the ramp, rolling onto the tile floor.

Opening the door, I saw a woman in her late 40s standing there. She looked athletic, wearing a T-shirt, bicycling shorts and biking shoes. Leaning against the wall was her bike. *I hope she's not selling something.*

"Kate? You don't know me. I'm Mary from church and I have been praying for you. May I come in?" she asked. I nodded silently and wheeled myself back down the ramp. She followed me into the kitchen and pulled a chair out for herself.

"You do very well with the wheelchair," she said sitting down.

"Well, I've had lots of practice," I replied.

"Kate, I wanted to come by sooner. Actually, I asked the pastor to deliver this. He felt I should come by myself," she said handing me something. It was a gold medal attached to a long blue ribbon. *A medal?*

Mary continued, "I felt bad when I heard what had happened to you. I knew you were an athlete. I used to see you working out at the gym. I prayed and felt inspired to run a triathlon in your honor. During the race I just kept praying, talking to God and to you, 'Kate, you've got to make it! You have to do this! Fight Kate!' 'I'm going to win this for Kate,' I kept telling myself."

I sat speechless, listening to her story. Mary proceeded, "I had to win, but I wanted to quit. My legs were tired and my feet were killing me. I knew I had to cross that finish line. Halfway through the race, I told a man who was running next to me that I had to win, and why. He said I should win for Kate, and not to give up. Tears were rolling down my cheeks as I crossed the finish line in first place." Mary sat back in the chair, taking a deep breath.

Wow. This is amazing! I sat there in stunned silence, clutching the medal. A chill ran down my spine. "This means a lot to me. Thank you. I'm a little overwhelmed right now and don't know what to say."

Patting me on the hand she said, "Well, I finally got up the courage to bring it by. I'm glad you are finally home and on the road to recovery." As she spoke, I was reminded of the verse in 2nd Timothy: "I have fought the good fight, I have finished the race, and I have kept the faith." *She has finished her race. I have only just begun. Maybe this medal will help me stay focused on that.*

"Thank you, Mary, thank you," I said seeing her to the door.

"Bye, Kate, I'll be praying for you," Mary said giving me a warm hug. *My story has touched a lot of people. I can make a difference. I wish I hadn't gone through all this suffering, but maybe I can use it for good. Thank you, God, for giving me a second chance.*

Chapter Sixteen

～

Back in the Driver's Seat

$\mathcal{M}$y attitude began to slowly improve. I was faced with many challenges that could not have been anticipated when I first dreamed of being home. Compared to where I had been for the past several months, my daughters and husband had been like a breath of fresh air. Despite the problems I was having with Steven and the household, I was glad to be home.

As time went on, however, the breath of fresh air began to feel more like a tornado. I resented all the work involved in raising two small children, taking care of a husband and recovering. Just to brush my teeth took determination and strategy. Depending on others was extremely difficult for this once independent girl. I couldn't even drive myself to therapy. My need for independence grew into an obsession.

The turning point in my recovery came when I could drive again. It had been six months since my stroke and I wasn't seeing any progress. Feeling depressed, I needed a milestone and expressed to my therapist my desire to drive. "I want to drive again," I told her. "I'm tired of relying on other people. I must have some independence."

"Okay Kate, we'll test you on Monday. Diane Chavez will be testing you," Susie said. *Really? That simple? I'm nervous, but thrilled.* She continued, "Freeman Hospital has their own driving evaluation that meets DMV standards."

I practiced driving with Steven that weekend, leaving the girls with the nanny so I could concentrate. We went to a large parking lot and I got into the driver's seat. *This feels great!* It felt natural, even though the left side of my body was partially paralyzed. (Of course, if the car had been a stick shift I could not have managed.) I drove confidently around, and instead of letting Steven take the wheel, I kept on driving out of the lot and all the way home. *Yes! I'm ready to drive.*

"Good job Kate, I think you will have no problem. Now, you'll be able to drive yourself to therapy," he said.

I remember being nervous Monday morning when I came to therapy. My two hours of therapy were spent evaluating my progress.

"Ready?" Diane asked coming to get me.

"Yes." I said enthusiastically.

"First, I need to go over a few basic rules before we do the actual road test," she said. *Rules? I know how to drive.* I followed her in my wheelchair and we went into a small room.

"Okay, I need to do a series of tests and I'll be timing you," Diane said. *Tests? I hate tests. I survived a stroke, isn't that enough?* She saw my look of apprehension, "Don't worry Kate, you'll do fine. These just tell me how quick your response is."

Diane had a sequence of tests involving cognitive testing, visual perception, and reaction time. She had me cover one eye while reading an eye chart. A machine with traffic lights tested my reaction time as the lights moved from green to amber to red.

"How am I doing?" I asked.

"Fine. We have one more test to do," she said. The test was to see how my eyes reacted to light for night driving. She turned off the lights in the room. "Kate, some lights will appear shining toward you for five seconds. You have one to three seconds to react," she said.

"Okay, I'm ready." I said.

She ran the test. "Good Kate, I think we are ready for the road test," she said switching the lights on. *Good. That's over.*

The final hour involved the actual road test. Diane wheeled my chair to the street level where the car was parked.

"How am I going to manage putting the wheelchair in my car?" I asked her.

"Someone will help you, but you are learning to use a walker, right?" she asked.

"Yes," I said as I transferred from the wheelchair to the driver's seat.

Diane explained everything while in the car. "This is a dual-equipped vehicle, so if you feel nervous, I can take over," she said.

"What is that funny looking thing?" I asked.

"That is called a steering wheel knob. It helps you turn corners using one hand," she said.

"I'm going to need one of those?"

"Believe me, you'll love it. It will come in handy. You're probably too young to remember, but years ago, truckers had them and so did teenagers. They were called 'necking knobs' but now they are illegal unless you have a physical need," she said. *Well, I don't plan on driving trucks or necking with anyone!*

I glanced around the car and adjusted the mirrors. With my good hand, I struggled to click the seat belt in place. *This will take some getting used to with one hand.* As I turned the key, I saw a long, thin piece of metal sticking out from the side of the wheel. "And this?" I asked.

"That's a turn signal when you want to change lanes," she said. *That's good. Somebody thought of everything.*

Cautiously, I drove the surface streets to my house. "I'd like to stop by and see the girls and grab my sunglasses if you don't mind," I asked her.

"You're the driver," Diane answered laughing.

We stopped by the house briefly. The girls were surprised to see me.

"Mom, what are you doing here?" Stephanie asked, puzzled.

"Your mom is learning to drive," Diane told her.

"Please let me come, please," Stephanie pleaded.

"No, I need to concentrate. Soon, Honey," I told her.

The nanny helped get the girls, and we left. Diane suggested we take the freeway back to the hospital. *Take the freeway?*

"Are you sure I'm ready for that?" I asked.

"There's only one way to find out. I wouldn't suggest it if I didn't feel comfortable," she said. I did fine driving on the freeway feeling confident using the steering knob; it helped especially with turning tight corners. We pulled up at the hospital and I parked the car.

"Well Kate, you did great and have passed the driving evaluation," she said.

"That's it?" I asked her.

"The only apparatus you'll need is a steering wheel knob and a turn signal, but otherwise you are ready," she said. *This is great! I needed this milestone.* "I will give the information to Dr. Alexander, who has the final say. I strongly recommend you don't drive until you get the equipment," she advised. *I can't wait to drive. I want to do it now.*

Steven drove my car the next day to have the apparatus put on.

"I want to drive myself to therapy. I'll take your car," I told him.

"Are you sure?" he asked.

"Yes, I'll be fine taking surface streets," I reassured him.

"What about the wheelchair?" he asked.

"I'll use my walker this morning. I have to practice anyway." The sense of freedom felt wonderful. I was on cloud nine. I turned the volume up on the radio, singing cheerfully to the music. *This feels great! I feel normal again.*

I was in therapy when Diane came up to me. "Hi Kate, how did you get to therapy this morning? Did someone drive you?" she asked. *Why is she asking me that? Did she see me?*

"Yes, I got here okay," I responded slyly.

"You didn't know that was me in front of you this morning, did you?" she said laughing.

"You were?" I said shocked. *Oh my gosh. She saw me driving.*

Diane grinned, "Yes, you couldn't wait to drive, even without your equipment on the car?" *Okay, so she caught me. I can't believe she was in front of me.*

"Steven drove the car to have the equipment put on. I wanted to drive so badly," I told her. "I was watching you, and you looked like you were doing fine," Diane said. All of us laughed and I went back to concentrating on therapy.

Of course, one of my first driving outings was to the mall. I remember driving up to the valet. "Hi, would you mind helping me?" I pulled the latch for the trunk. "I need help with my wheelchair," I said. The valet assembled my chair and I proudly wheeled myself into the mall. *This feels great! I can go shopping on my own.*

Driving is important to stroke survivors. It is not merely a luxury to drive, but a necessity. Many survivors become filled with fear at the thought of learning to drive again. Can I do this? What if I don't succeed? Should I even bother trying?

It's wonderful, however, to see the changed attitude of a stroke survivor who can drive again. The late Charlie Corn helped many survivors accomplish this important goal.

"Almost anyone can drive," he said. "They just have to compensate for their problems with the right adaptive equipment. It's also important to have training in safe driving."

Every DMV office has a driver safety program for anyone with a medical problem. Some applicants, who have been driving for years prior to their stroke, assume they will have no trouble passing the test. The regulatory test runs 25 minutes, and the driver safety officer has been specially trained on how to test these applicants. Things covered in the test are: vision perception, reaction time, functional ability and the actual on-the-road test.

Sometimes, the applicant has a lengthy waiting period for the results. Today, with more drivers on the road, raised speed limits, and large trucks, it's important to have driver safety programs available. In order to feel comfortable and confident with the adaptive equipment, training is necessary.

Now that I was home, I took a greater interest in my appearance. The first thing I decided to do was have my hideous brace cut down so it wouldn't be noticeable. I discussed it with my therapist who sent me to see Michael Jefferies.

"Are you sure you want me to do that?" he asked.

"Yes, I'm positive. I don't want people staring at my brace," I said. *I hope I'm doing the right thing. I know it will look better.*

"You won't have the knee control," Michael replied.

"The knee control will be fine," I said. The brace was cut so it sat midway at my calf.

After several years, and several near mishaps, I had a new brace made, one that came back up to my knee. The brace keeps my knee from snapping back. By wearing long pants, no one could see my brace. It has taken me this long to feel comfortable enough to wear the brace and not be concerned what people think.

Funny, I was more concerned about how I looked than whether I could walk. As I look back, I have to laugh at myself. I remember one day going into outpatient rehab with a beautiful pair of shoes, trying to convince my therapist that I could wear them. Sitting in my wheelchair, I held up the shoes.

"Look, Herlene, aren't these beautiful?" I took off my tennis shoes and struggled to put on the fancy dress heels. I squeezed my brace into the left shoe, feeling like one of Cinderella's sisters. I adjusted the straps and sat back exhausted, but proud. I had them on. The shoes were all heel and straps.

"I could have the heel cut down," I said pensively.

"Yes Kate, they certainly are beautiful," Herlene said with an unreadable expression. *I can tell she knows these won't work.*

"Doesn't my right foot look sexy in these?" I asked, hoping for some miraculous way to wear them and walk.

Herlene laughed, "Kate, they are fine looking shoes. Of course you can wear them. You'll have to give up walking, but you can wear them. Your choice."

The shoes were returned to the store and replaced with a simpler style.

I love shoes. I am a shoe hog. I have always had dozens of pairs. When you suddenly go from stylish to basic, flat, matronly Velcro practical, it is a real downer.

As the saying goes, "If the shoe fits, wear it." So heels are history!

I still don't want to look like a geek, and finding a pair of shoes that is attractive yet functional with a brace is not an easy task. Even today, I longingly look at other women's shoes wishing I could wear them. When I have those thoughts, I simply remember when shoes weren't the issue but taking my first step was. That seems to put shoes – and life – in perspective.

I felt ready to talk with others about my stroke. My friend, Jenny, agreed to drive me to a stroke support meeting. I had previously attended a couple of other groups but found I couldn't relate. I was much younger, with two small children and the issues that go along with being a young wife and mother.

I soon warmed up to a new group that was for stroke survivors 55 and under. It was there that I met another courageous stroke survivor, Candace. She had started a support group so I asked her how she got it going. As we talked, she encouraged me to start one in my area and referred me to the Stroke Association of California's then Executive Director Susan Blatt, for guidance. I wanted to use my experience to make a difference, and helping others like me seemed a good idea. I was excited to get going. The woman told me to find a location and get back to them.

I called some hospitals to inquire about starting a group. One woman asked, "What are your credentials?" *Credentials? No one knows more about a stroke than me. I've lived through it.*

"I've survived a stroke," I replied. The woman mentioned someone from administration would get back to me.

Sometimes they did and sometimes they didn't. When they did, I usually heard that discouraging word – no. You have to be willing to hear no in order to get a yes.

Stroke survivors know that we don't always get information right. I must have had that problem because whenever I heard the word *no,* somehow I misunderstood and thought I heard *keep trying.*

One day I met with an administrator from Beach Cities Hospital and convinced her there was a need for a stroke support group. We talked over details and my persistence paid off. The Back on Track group was founded. Starting the group gave me a sense of independence and self-esteem. I had flyers made and posted them all over my community. The word spread and the group began to grow. By reaching out and helping others, I helped myself on my own journey to recovery.

The executive director, Susan, was pleased that a new support group had been started. She asked if I would like to help out by raising funds for their health fair. The Stroke Association was having their annual health fair soon with a 5K walk/run. I felt honored to help out. I suggested to her that since I had small children, it would be great to have one of those huge inflatable bouncers for kids.

"Well, we really don't have many kids at the event," Susan replied.

"Young people have strokes, and I'm sure a lot of these people attending must have kids and grandchildren," I responded.

"That's something I'll bring up to the board. In the meantime, I'd love you to sell some raffle tickets and maybe get together a team," she said.

I ended the phone call telling her I'd come by her office to pick up some tickets. That next morning, Susan handed me a stack of raffle tickets to sell on their behalf. I organized a team of walkers and we enthusiastically started selling tickets.

I was excited to raise money for the organization and decided I would hold a bake sale at my house. I rented a Cinderella Castle bouncer and had it set up in my backyard. I had many friends with small children and knew it would be a great little fund-raiser. We charged parents a dollar to let their kids play in the bouncer.

Friends volunteered to bake cookies, brownies, muffins and cakes. We advertised widely through posters and flyers.

I was in outpatient therapy and that week I focused on my cooking ability to make banana bread. Mum had given me a wonderful no-fail recipe for banana bread years ago. It was the one and only cake I could bake well.

In outpatient therapy, there was a small kitchen off to the side where patients learned to cook. Not only did I do a lot of reaching in the cupboards for ingredients, but I also had to concentrate on the rest of my body.

My therapist stayed by my side while I stood trying to bear weight on my leg. Focusing on my posture, I squeezed my butt and stomach tight, while keeping my shoulder blades squeezed. I had to be aware that my arm wasn't hanging limp. It was difficult to stir the mixture with one good arm and think of all these things at the same time. While the cake was baking, I cleaned up my mess (at the request of my therapist). Just doing that simple task was more therapy.

Kate's former support group

Before long, the aroma of the baking bread filled the kitchen and therapy room. The therapists popped their heads in the kitchen to see if the bread was ready. *There has to be a way I can raise money here. That's what I'll do. I'll sell slices of hot banana bread to the therapists.*

I baked banana bread that entire week, selling warm slices for a dollar.

I held the fund-raiser at my home with friends stopping by. Children loved jumping in the bouncer as their parents donated money for the Stroke Association.

Mum's Famous Banana Bread

1 egg
1 cup sugar
1-3/4 cup flour
1 teaspoon baking powder
4 ounces butter
2 mashed bananas (the older the better – within reason!)
1 teaspoon baking soda dissolved in 1/2 c milk (added last)

Cream butter and sugar until light and fluffy add egg and beat. Using a wooden spoon, gradually fold in flour, baking powder and mashed bananas. Then add soda and milk. Bake in a loaf tin approximately 50-60 minutes at 350°.

Happy baking!

Monday morning I brought $1,000 in cash to the Stroke Association office. Susan was thrilled (actually she was shocked). "This is wonderful, Kate, I would love to clone about ten of you."

Before the big health fair, Susan asked me if I'd like to be a director on the board. I could meet many of the board members at the event. The day of the event, I proudly wore a ribbon with the word "Director" printed on it. It was a great morning, with many walkers and runners out raising money for the cause.

Becoming a director with the Stroke Association gave me the opportunity to help others while I was still in therapy. *I'm back in the driver's seat.* I was extremely happy.

Another fund-raising project I helped coordinate was a fashion show, with Nordstrom as the sponsor. I had been a frequent shopper there before my stroke and knew many of the salespeople. While raising money for the health fair, I had asked them to sponsor me. Someone suggested that I submit my story to their corporate office on behalf of the Stroke Association, so I did. Now, I waited anxiously for their response.

I approached the Stroke Association at a board meeting and told them of my idea. They gave me their blessings with a moderate amount of enthusiasm.

I worked closely with Nordstrom, attending several fashion shows to see how they were organized. I submitted more than 400 names of my own friends and contacts to the Association for my list of invitees. We were scheduled for an April fashion show, and Nordstrom did an outstanding job of securing the models.

As the guests arrived, they were greeted and given a light buffet breakfast. The stage was in place and the runway show was amazing, with beautiful models showing the latest spring fashions. The fashion show was a huge financial success. Not only was a significant sum of money raised, the event also helped raise awareness of stroke and stroke prevention.

These two events were the start of my fund-raising activities for the Stroke Association. I became active as a director on the board, attending numerous health fairs on behalf of the organization.

My story was going to be featured in an upcoming issue of *Stroke Connection,* a national magazine published by the American Heart Association. The Heart Association held their annual International Joint Conference on Stroke in California, February 1996. I received a call from Elizabeth, a staff member from the magazine, who was working on the article asking me to come to Anaheim and deliver a short speech.

"Kate, this would be great if you would speak. That way everyone will be able to put a name to the face when the article comes out," she told me.

Not knowing what to expect, I said, "Okay, I'll do it." *I haven't spoken publicly before, except to a few stroke groups. I hope it's not a lot of people.*

Arriving at the conference I met Elizabeth who hurried me into the room where the luncheon was taking place. I gasped at the number of people sitting at tables.

"Here Kate, let's sit you here," she said. She then introduced me to each person at the table. *I'm going to speak before this many people?*

"How many people are in this room?" I asked.

"Oh, this is an annual International Stroke Conference with about 1,800 attendees including neurologists, surgeons, physicians and nurses in the field of strokes," she said.

"And I'm going to speak before them?" I asked nervously.

"Don't worry, you'll do fine. They will love you and before they leave here today your name will be a household word."

Elizabeth helped me onto the stage. I stood behind the podium with my legs shaking and my heart pounding. *You can do this. Just stay calm.* As I spoke, you could have heard a pin drop. I began feeling at ease standing up there. The 10 minutes I was allotted went by quickly and the crowd broke into applause as I left the stage. *That went well!*

As I sat down at my table, I realized that I could make a difference in other people's lives. *I can help someone else who is hurting. I can help them on their journey, by sharing mine.*

"Great job Kate. That was wonderful!" Elizabeth exclaimed, "Kirk Douglas couldn't have done better."

"Kirk Douglas?" I asked.

"Yes, we were trying to get him to speak but he wasn't available," she said. *How exciting! I was Kirk Douglas' replacement.*

From the Other Side of the Bed

*K*ate had found her voice and her cause. At first, I think her desire to speak publicly was partly catharsis and partly wanting to help others. As time went on, the balance would shift almost completely toward helping others.

As much as I admired what Kate was doing, there was also a cost. Kate had a new purpose in life, it seemed, and I felt it began to replace me.

I eventually came to understand that Kate's healing from her trauma was enhanced by her helping others in similar circumstances. At that time I did not understand what was happening.

The stats are not good for marriage after stroke. Ninety percent of the couples break up. Kate and I thought we would be the exception, yet we were talking less and less to each other. I don't know why, but we could not see our own problems. It was like being in the forest and not able to see the trees. I did not know what to do.

I was sure we had something special that other couples didn't. I spent a lot of time with Kate as she developed her support group and got to know all of the participants. In one situation, the husband had aphasia and mild cognitive problems. It looked like they would make a go of it but, one day, the wife drove him to her mother in law's home. "He is your problem now," she said – and that was that.

The wife was not a bad person, she just had enough. They had only been married a couple of years before his stroke. I could not help but think that "until death do us part" came a tad too early.

I knew that no matter what, I would stick with Kate. I felt in my heart that marriage was sacred and should not be dissolved because of inconvenience – even if it was a *catastrophic inconvenience. I could not say I was happy, but that was not the issue.*

I may have had the right opinion about marriage, however I was no longer communicating with Kate. As she stepped out more and more to heal from her trauma by helping others, she stepped further and further away from me and the girls.

She was learning about herself – by herself – which ultimately she had to, And how to live with severe disabilities. I had saved her life, but I could not heal the catastrophic wounds Kate endured because of her stroke. I was no longer needed as her advocate. I was no longer her hero. Kate was on her way up and I was on my way down.

With no real support, or even understanding what I was going through, I was hitting rock bottom. There is more than one victim of stroke. It affects the whole family. I just didn't realize how much. I was very, very sad.

Kate had a catastrophic trauma, which meant starting over. Even after coming home, she had reduced physical abilities. She could not walk, or take care of herself without assistance. Her daughters were too young to understand why they could not get what they needed from her. They needed her more, not less, after having suffered this traumatic separation, and so did I.

Kate needed to put all her energy into healing and redefining who she was. She had survived and what she needed now was to bring meaning, validity and focus to her life as a severely disabled person, and she did.

I soon began speaking nationally on behalf of the American Heart Association (AHA). I spoke at local support groups and furthered my speaking interest by joining the local chapter of the National Speakers Association. There, I met others who encouraged and supported me as I developed my speaking business. I decided to become a board member with my local AHA division, involving my daughters in events to raise money.

November 1997, a new nationwide division of the AHA was established for stroke survivors. It was named the American Stroke Association (ASA). I began to speak at various affiliates throughout the country. I was asked to testify before the United States Congress, to help gain more funds for stroke and heart research. (My speech is reprinted in the appendix.)

I remember that trip to Washington and how I felt in the courtroom. The chamber was packed with reporters and television cameras. There were bright lights and clicking of cameras. There wasn't a seat left in the room. My husband wheeled me in, maneuvering the chair into a corner. *Why is it so busy in here?*

"That's Muhammad Ali sitting there," he whispered. *The real Muhammad Ali? Why is he here?* I listened closely as I heard his wife testifying for him on behalf of the Parkinson's Disease Society. After her speech, she escorted him out, trailed by eager reporters and cameramen. *I'm glad I don't have that size of audience listening to me.*

It was my turn to speak. I was seated at the table to read my speech. I had exactly five minutes before a gong was sounded. The speech had been carefully looked over, and edited somewhat, by the AHA people.

I was suddenly nervous. After all, I was speaking before Congress. *Calm down. These people are human just like me. There's nothing to be afraid of.* I was familiar with my speech, but I read every word, occasionally looking up. I was relieved when it was over.

Also in 1997, I spoke in Washington at a live press conference at the National Mall in front of the Capitol. I shared the podium with Senator Barbara Boxer and other representatives. Several speakers were there with me to help launch the AHA campaign, "Take Wellness to Heart." Behind the stage in the shape of the AHA logo were thousands of red and white carnations. The floral tribute covered the size of a football field. Cranes were available to allow aerial photos. This served as a memorial to the half a million women who die of cardiovascular disease each year. (More women die of strokes than breast cancer.)

I was proud to be a part of this important campaign to help reach other women. This speech wasn't off the cuff. I had specific points to be covered. It was windy that morning and as I watched the other speakers, I suddenly realized that they have two hands to hold their notes. *How am I going to be able to hold my notes and turn the pages in this wind.* I advised the AHA staff of the problem (otherwise I would have been left quite speechless as my notes flew through the air). A folder was quickly devised that I could tuck each page in as I read.

That day, I began to accept my disability. Acknowledging that I may never completely recover was one of the hardest things I have had to come to terms with.

～

I find that children are not afraid to ask direct questions. When Stephanie was in the first grade, her teacher gave the children an assignment to write what was special about their parents and to draw a picture. Stephanie asked her daddy to help. It said:

"My mom is special because she did not die from her stroke. My little sister thinks Mom had a stroke because she ate too much candy. I help Mom walk and rest her dead arm on my shoulder."

She wrote that, along with a drawing of me with a missing arm.

Once a week I helped out in Stephanie's classroom. The teacher never gave me anything I couldn't handle. I assisted with reading and oversaw their coloring assignments. Stephanie had a show and tell where she talked about my experience. I didn't find out until the following week. When I walked into the room, all the children ran up to me. *What a greeting.*

They were intrigued and eager to see my dead arm that Stephanie had told them about. "What happened to your arm?" "Why do you walk like that?"

"Oh, my mom had a stroke," Stephanie replied.

"What's a stroke?" they asked.

"It means her arm and leg don't work," she said.

The children stared at me in bewilderment. *Kids will be kids!*

Steven and Kate

Chapter Seventeen

~

Lessons Learned

$\mathcal{T}$ he weeks turned into months, and with the rising pressure on me, I found myself returning to some support groups. The girls were doing well. My pressure now came from being overwhelmed with adjusting to my new physical limitations and life in general. Even with my new sense of purpose, I was unhappy in my marriage. How could I be happy? I still suffered from emotional lability and depression. I couldn't effectively use much of the left side of my body. I couldn't walk without a brace and I didn't feel that I really knew who I was. I felt inadequate.

It was at the support meetings I met a man who appeared to have all I wanted. He was a single man, without kids, who wanted me for me, and would provide a space where I could be myself without a care in the world – or so I thought.

My marriage was in trouble. I resented the family needing me to be there for them like I was before when I was whole and healthy. I was almost dead not long ago, and was a long way from full recovery, yet it seemed for them, life was business as usual and I was expected to take care of them – just as before. I had been through too much, and I wanted to be responsible only for me. I was lost and overwhelmed.

I was not thinking clearly when I decided to file for a divorce in November of 1998.

From the Other Side of the Bed

I was, of course, totally against the divorce. It made no sense to me. Looking back years later, it still makes no sense. Of course, there are always signs but I just didn't want to see them. I had many chances to address the problem, yet made the choice not to. I got angrier and angrier.

I was resentful that Kate was not showing me more gratitude. I thought I should have been given a medal. No, I thought I should have been given ten medals. So there we were, Kate could stay home to deal with a spouse who was constantly asking for more and more attention. Or she could leave to help others and/or spend time with a man who would tell her anything to convince her that he was wonderful and that I was awful. What a mess we created.

Kate's new relationship was with a man without honor. Don't get me wrong, a wife who is well taken care of usually does not stray. I played a part in our break up. I made the foolish choice of keeping my pride rather than keeping my wife. That was my mistake. Put the whole package together, and we had a recipe for our marriage failing; hurt feelings, deep sorrow and regret.

It is not surprising that Kate and I were no longer attending church together on a regular basis. If we had stayed connected with the church, I truly believe that we would never have gotten a divorce. The Bible is clear that God hates divorce. No one looking at divorce wants to stay too close to God. We tell ourselves that our new love must be from God because we are so happy. Or, we are right and won't pay attention to our spouse's needs or wants. It is our will, not God's will.

When you add bad ideas on both sides to two stubborn and prideful hearts, you have a train wreck. That is what happened to us. We paid a high and bitter price.

Separating from Steven was a mistake. It is through our mistakes and through forgiving ourselves and others we learn to grow and move on.

Over the past few years, I have learned many lessons. While I was away from my family, I realized how important it was to be a full time mum. I hated being separated from my daughters during those important growing-up years. I missed the companionship of my best friend, Steven. True, our relationship was far from perfect, but he was my safety net.

The stroke was not just a physical event, it was also an emotional and spiritual blow. First, the stroke hit me physically. I had to adjust to a body that functioned differently. I now had new limitations to deal with. I lost my sense of who I was. I no longer knew how to be Kate. I had been in perfect physical shape, now, parts of my body no longer functioned. Everything was totally unfamiliar and awkward. Life was overwhelming. I was a different person. I had been shattered. Now I had to rebuild. No one understood, and frankly, neither did I.

My marriage was wrecked. I wasn't the only victim of my stroke. But, I was a victim, and I needed to be away from the pressure of dealing with my family's constant needs. I was in no way physically or emotionally capable of fulfilling their needs. I felt alone, with no support.

I could see no way out except – out. I felt it would take a greater miracle to restore the marriage than the one that had restored my health and mobility. I was emotionally and spiritually exhausted. I could not see the tiny green shoots that would eventually push their way through the charred wreckage of my life.

While my divorce was moving through the system, I learned we could have the status of the marriage dissolved, yet leave the other issues to be decided later. That is what we did.

After a few months of arguing and trips in and out of court, Steven got full custody of the girls, with my rights limited to supervised visits because of my physical limitations.

At first, the girls visited me in my new home. It was awkward and sad, mostly because of my (new) husband's attitude toward my children. Weekend visits went by quickly. Then I was left with five more days in a world I didn't understand with a new husband who didn't understand either. Where I was living was okay, but far away from everything familiar to me.

Tension with my daughters grew because of my new relationship. It was difficult for them to accept me being with anyone other than their father.

Unlike Steven, my new husband (we will call him Bruce) did recognize how fragile I was, and used it against me. He did everything he could to destroy my relationship with my children and Steven. I nearly lost my children entirely. Bruce didn't understand them, didn't like them, and wished I didn't have them. He had no children and wanted us to be just us. He often lost his temper with my daughters. He made negative comments about their dad, which they took back home. This all caused tremendous tension for everyone. He kept telling me everything would be fine if I would just let them go.

"Everything would be fine if you didn't have kids," he'd tell me.

"Well I do, and I am their mother," I repeatedly told him. "Furthermore, no matter what, Steven is their dad and he'll always be around. If you want me, you are stuck with them."

I had lost who I was in the emotional chaos. I finally realized that I needed to muster all the courage I could and call for professional help. This was a huge risk, because it meant exposing the truth and I didn't even know what that truth was. It meant exposing myself and I didn't know who I was. I knew I had to take that risk if I was to survive.

From the Other Side of the Bed

I had no idea what was going on. I thought Kate had no interest in her children. I did not realize that she was in an abusive relationship. I knew Kate as a strong and capable woman. I had no idea how fragile she had become since her stroke.

Because I did not know Kate was trapped in an abusive relationship, I also made some bad decisions. I made things worse by using my legal expertise to have my way in the divorce. I thought I was doing the right thing for my children, and I was, but only in that they needed to be protected from Kate's new partner.

I ultimately wound up with a restraining order against him which forbade him from being within 100 feet of the children. Sadly, I did not realize that Kate was not the problem. I made it hard for her to see the children. That was a big mistake.

To Kate's credit, she stood up to every obstacle I put in her way. She clung to her children with a death grip. In the end it was Bruce's demand that she never see her children that ended their relationship.

I had been representing myself in court. I did not have the funds to keep hiring attorneys. The Superior Court of Los Angeles is a scary place if you aren't familiar with the legal system. Speaking in court was fine, except I did not know the legal system well enough to be representing myself.

I was in the middle of a war, but in reality Steven never really went after me. He loved his daughters immensely, and it showed. He was very protective of them so he fought for them. He also wanted me back and fought all the harder to have custody of the girls because he knew they were a long-term link to me. He applied the same tenacity he used to fight for my life to fight for custody of the girls. Steven is an excellent attorney and represented his position well. I was my own worst enemy, as are most people who represent themselves. My physical and emotional condition didn't help. The truth was, with my obvious disability, I was simply not able to care for my daughters full time. The outcome was predictable.

Oddly, Steven refused to accept that a civil court could grant a divorce. It is a religious thing with him. Even though we were now legally divorced, he refused to recognize the divorce process. He continually demanded that we reconcile. I don't do well when someone demands I do something. Steven was trying to bring us together but he was pushing us further and further apart.

We had both exhausted our financial resources as a result of my stroke, now the little we had left was consumed in legal costs, to wage a fight that no one wanted. Both of us are stubborn.

I did not know who to trust. Everyone had a different story to tell. My girlfriends, for the most part, supported me. I never stopped being grateful for the love and support my husband and daughters had given me, but somehow I linked my depression to them. I had clearly survived my stroke, but had not recovered from the damage which was not just physical. I sometimes took my anger and frustration out on those closest to me. Getting away from them was, I thought, the solution. I guess there is some truth in the old expression, "you only hurt the people you love," and I hurt myself worse in the process.

Before this sorry chapter in our lives was over, my family and I would lose all of what remained of our life together. We lost material items, and more importantly suffered harm to our family; emotionally, spiritually, and psychologically.

Now slowly began the unfolding of another miracle, the ultimate restoration of my marriage and family. It certainly has not been an easy process. It has taken years to deal with the struggle, the pain, the changes and learning to trust again. Not just me learning to trust, but also my children and Steven. In fact, trust is probably the biggest loss we have experienced and the most difficult to reestablish.

I was estranged from the people I loved most, and distrustful of the man who had fought so hard to save my life. Every day I seemed to get more depressed and irrational. I was adrift in a storm, not knowing how to restore what was lost. Unrelenting feelings of guilt and inadequacy haunted me.

Even if I could have, I did not want to restore the past. I felt that I had suffered much and deserved something for myself. It is very common for people who have been through a serious illness to feel this way. I was so damaged that I felt I had nothing to give my children or Steven.

He continued to refuse to acknowledge that our divorce was valid. He insisted that he loved me and always would. Steven told me that for him marriage was eternal, and no matter what, he was my husband.

One of the best decisions I made was to seek outside help and start working through my feelings. I missed the girls terribly. The more Steven insisted we should get back together, the more I resisted. It was a door I wanted to go back through, but like most people, I don't like being pushed.

It wasn't necessary for Steven and me to be fighting. After three law firms and huge legal expenses, I finally found a divorce attorney who agreed that we should work this out amicably, and was interested in the children's welfare. He set the foundation for reestablishing the relationship with my family and was skilled enough to navigate through the legal system making sure that everyone was protected. In a few short weeks he got both parties communicating with each other. This was such a blessing.

Around Thanksgiving, 2000, things began to change for us. Steven went through all kinds of trouble to find a last minute turkey. He found a local restaurant that was willing, at an extra cost, to make a full-blown turkey dinner.

Here I was with my family again, or was it my family? It had been three years since all of us sat down and gave thanks together. I could see that here was something real, a tie that winds of circumstances had not changed.

Earlier that week, Bruce had presented me with an ultimatum. He demanded that I choose him or my children. Who did he think he was? I may have been out of my mind, but I would never be that crazy. I don't see how any mother could make that kind of choice. Talking with my therapist helped immensely, but I always knew what my choice would be.

Shortly after Christmas, I moved into a small guest house in Manhattan Beach to be near Steven and the girls. It's not like things changed overnight. I knew in my heart the best thing for our family was somehow to be a family.

First, we agreed to make the children the focus of our lives and to try to do whatever was best for them. You don't have to be a rocket scientist to know what is best for children. Putting aside our resentments, we struggled to remain focused on raising the girls. This was another miracle for me, being a mom again.

When all is said and done, it's the kids that get hurt during divorce. Things are much better for all of us. I am there for Stephanie and Rachel. Having a mom and a dad again has made a huge impact on the girls. They are no longer shuffled back and forth between two arguing parents. Making the children our main priority has been the best decision we could have made.

I realized through this process; this is a man who truly does love me.

I love being a family again. We were able to let go of our anger and resentments. We all have our pluses and minuses. Though not really a fairy tale, we are really trying to live happily ever after.

From the Other Side of the Bed

On April 5, 2004, we were remarried. We chose that date because it was our original wedding anniversary. We think of ourselves as having been married for a number of years with a brief intermission.

Epilogue

If you are facing personal tragedy or other difficult circumstances, I encourage you to persist in your own journey until you triumph. I hope this book has helped put you in touch with how special you are and how your struggles can make a difference in others' lives. I pray my journey helps you realize you are on a unique path designed by God to strengthen your mind, body and soul.

Adversity can strike us at any time. For those who have not suffered a catastrophic adversity, maybe this will help you understand and respect others' suffering, and offer support or relief to those on a difficult journey.

Writing this book has been a deeply moving experience. To remember the details, I had to resurrect the nightmare. I had to remember how it feels to be kept alive by machines, treated like a vegetable, and talked about within earshot as if I were not there. I had to re-live being a viable consciousness, trapped in an essentially lifeless body, a vibrant soul attached to cold machines, turned every few hours.

I am still partially paralyzed on my left side with limited use of my left leg and no use of my left arm; however, I am alive. With the help of many, I have fought my way back from despair and immobility to an energetic and joyful new life, as a wife and mother. I am doing many things today that most people, including most medical professionals, thought would never again be possible for me.

From this hellish experience, my speaking and writing career was born. I have been blessed with new purpose. I have learned that every life, no matter how seemingly insignificant, is important and can make a difference.

We strive for easy lives and comfortable pleasures, but often the price for such ease and comfort is a weak spirit and hollow soul that could count for much more in the great scheme of life.

This is not just about my struggle, but also yours, and that of thousands of ordinary people who became extraordinary by dealing with circumstances that have been thrust upon them. My written story is about the power of prayer, faith and courage. So are the unwritten stories of many others.

Perhaps the greatest gift of my tragedy is the revelation that no matter the pain or problem, there is purpose; no matter the tragedy or trial, there is triumph.

May God Bless,
Kate Adamson

Acknowledgments

Many played a tremendous part in my recovery and as I continue on this journey called life, I offer many heartfelt thanks to:

My husband Steven, the love of my life, who went an infinite distance to save me.

Stephanie and Rachel, who showed amazing courage and resiliency. My parents and extended family in New Zealand who had faith in me during the early days of the unknown.

Dr. Jeffrey Saver and Dr. Helena Chui for their contributions; Dr. Stephen Kolodney, Dr. David Alexander, Dr. Judy Carl, Betsy Cogen, Physical Therapist, and all the medical professionals who believed in me, or simply suspended judgment so that miracles could happen.

Torrance Memorial and Centinela Freeman Hospitals where I regained my life.

Friends, family and all the other earthly angels who kept vigil through the night and treated me as a person when I didn't look like one. My Heavenly Father and his angels who watched over me and gave me back the miracle of life, and blesses me today with the privilege of blessing others with my story.

My colleagues with the National Speakers Association and others throughout the world who helped me write, speak, and stand on my own two feet again.

Darlyn Strawn for her efforts proofreading.

Editorial Assistants, Mary Elias and Beth Rhodes for getting to press on time.

Letters to Kate

I receive hundreds of letters every year, and every one of them is appreciated.

I thank those who have taken the time to write. These letters have helped me in my journey and dealing with all I have been through.

~

Kate, My father had his stroke on September 18th. They tell us he can definitely hear us and the surgeon believes he understands some commands. My greatest fear is that he is trapped inside his body and will remain in this state indefinitely... I read your story daily and it brings me great comfort. I refuse to give up hope even though I can see doctors losing hope... You didn't give up, and I feel my daddy has that same type of will to survive. Sincerely, M. Wright

~

Kate, Your story rang true to many of my thoughts and feelings, so I congratulate you on your ability to write in a way which allows your reader to relate. Thanks for being a wonderful role model and sharing so others like me can look up a little each day. M. Mohr

~

Hi Kate, I read your article in the October Issue of *Redbook*. You are an extremely brave woman, someone others who may suffer from the same or similar problem could look up to and gain hope from. Thank you, LM

~

Hi, I am a registered nurse in an emergency room and previously worked in a physical rehab unit. I was surprised at your story and wanted to congratulate you on your recovery. It is a very inspiring story and I will carry it around with me to show my coworkers. It will be an encouragement for everyone. M.

~

Dear Katie, Thank you for sharing your story. You truly are an inspiration. I sincerely feel a person's makeup, such as being passive or assertive, makes a definite difference in their recovery process. And also the type of family and support system a person has. Your family and community were wonderful. Carol, Niagara Falls, NY

~

Dear Kate, You are an inspiration. My on-line friend's husband just suffered a stroke in April. You give hope that there is a possibility of recovery for him. Each little thing he does is progress. I'm far from my friend, but I try to keep her spirits up. Thanks for your website. Joy

~

Kate, I am suffering the effects of a devastating stroke. I take comfort, during this extremely difficult time, knowing that someone understands what I am going through and being able to share my thoughts and feelings. Sincerely, J. Bellino

~

Dear Kate, I am studying to be a nurse.... There is a man in the ward I work in who also suffers from locked-in syndrome and to tell you the truth I feel very sorry for the pain he is going through. He is married with two lovely boys, and he is doing well. He had brainstem stroke and is paralyzed. He cries every day, wondering if he will ever recover; every day he is making wonderful progress because of you. Thank you for sharing your story and I hope some day this man will regain strength like you have. Yours sincerely, Pamela Mizzi, Malta, Europe

~

Dear Katie, I am a 30 year old Aussie who has just visited your website. Wow! Congratulations! While I know no two strokes are the same, your story is so similar to that of a very dear friend of mine who suffered a massive brainstem stroke. She is only 33 years old and has an 18-month-old daughter and a three-year-old son. It's now seven months later and she is able to spend the weekends at home with her family. Reading your story was like looking back at the last seven months. The best part was seeing where you are at now... Karen Maschek

~

Hi Katie, I read with great interest and admiration the article about you in *Redbook* magazine. You have been so brave throughout this entire ordeal and I know that you will someday walk again without the walker. B. Rammes

~

Katie, Your story is amazing! I had my stroke in July this year at the age of 26. Although I am making progress, it is very slow and frustrating. The doctors here in England don't know much about strokes and I still don't know what caused mine. I can walk with a cane but very slowly and can't move my left arm. Any advice on recovery would be appreciated. Best wishes, Michelle

~

Dear Kate, You have been such an inspiration to me. I could not begin to thank you enough. I had a hemorrhagic stroke (affecting my right side). I did NOT know you were NOT supposed to regain full function and I have way too much tenacity. I was even figuring how to get better in the ambulance going to the hospital. I've come an awful long way, all because of YOU! T. Cooper

~

Dear Kate, I am excited to see how you have brought so much blessing into the lives of others who have suffered strokes. I don't know if you remember me, I was in your Bible Study group on Tuesday mornings at Hope Chapel. Take care and God bless you and your family. Sincerely, Laura

~

Kate, Years ago, I had a stroke that caused speech difficulties, almost a total memory loss, difficulty in reading and writing, depression and general disorientation. My speech therapist recommended that my wife Gloria and I attend the Back on Track support group. A few years later, my wife Gloria who was my active care taker, had a massive hemorrhagic stroke [leaving] her with a totally paralyzed right side, and unable to talk, eat or drink. She spent 105 days in a rehabilitation facility before she was released in a wheelchair and needing constant care. During her time in the hospital and in the care center, we had many visits from you. As my wife improved we returned to a support group, now not only for me, but more for Gloria. These activities are a mainstay of her recovery. Henry Luhrs

Hello Kate, I too had a stroke (5 TIAs and 2 major paralyzing ones on my right side). I think I'll enjoy each day for what it is! Now my goal is to help others in any way that I can. I'm glad I found you and maybe, who knows someday, sometime, somewhere, we will meet. It is sure wonderful to know that there are others like you out there who remain so positive after all that has happened! God Bless you and your family. Cheryl

Dear Kate, Your story in *Redbook* was powerful and much needed for me as my dad just had a stroke. He is not able, at this time, to move his left side. To make it a bit more intense, the day he was brought into the hospital, he was given TPA, which caused massive bleeding in his neck. He has a trachea from the surgery and is unable to speak – Thank you so much for giving me hope. H.

Dear Kate, I read your article in *Redbook* and I was terrified. I have suffered severe migraines since I was 13 years old. Two years ago, I was going to sleep when I lost all the feeling in the left side of my body and I was in terrible pain. For the next several weeks, I could barely talk or walk. My GP told me that it was psychological. Six months ago, I saw a neurologist that specializes in migraines and he informed me that the experience that I had was a direct result of my migraines. Thank you for being an inspiration to everyone that reads about your experience. K. Walsh

Ms. Kate, Your story overwhelmed me, brought tears to my eyes and has made me realize how much harder I have to fight. My mother had a severe stroke. They told my father and me she had a slim chance of survival. We put our lives on hold and gave complete unconditional love and time to my mother. She left a rehab center and can communicate fairly well. She still has no movement in her right hand or arm, but is able to walk on her own (with a cane and brace) and can talk 40% of the time with full sentences. Since I read your article, I think of you and what you must have gone through. Thank you. T. Murray

Dear Katie, I wanted to take a moment to tell you that when I finished reading the article in *Redbook*, I thanked God for your husband's persistence and love for you. I admire your courage and fortitude. You must have been very, very frightened, unable to communicate, not fully understanding what had happened to you. You are a remarkable woman, and I wish you the best that life has to offer. I have a twenty-month-old daughter myself and even though I have full use of both of my arms, I still cannot put her hair up in a pony tail (she won't hold still long enough!). May God bless and keep you and yours safe. Sincerely, S. Cooper

Dear Kate, After reading your wonderful story, my family and I were overwhelmed with new hope for our sister. There was much spirit and courage depicted in your message, it has renewed our faith that there may be some hope of some recovery for her, She has locked-in syndrome. She can only move her eyes to communicate. She has indicated to us that she feels things, but can't move. The doctors say she will probably not get any better, but we refuse to accept that. Thank you again for having the courage to come forth. Sincerely, D. Williams

Appendix

~

For Other Stroke Survivors

Often people contact me regarding a loved one who has had a stroke, asking for advice. I am not a medical professional and, therefore, am only offering encouragement and hope.

Unfortunately, there is no magical pill that brings us back to a fully functioning life. The process is slow, and we don't usually see the gains immediately. The best solution is a lot of hard work and even more patience.

It is important to remember that no two strokes are the same. Every stroke patient reacts and recovers in a different way. It's best not to compare. There is light at the end of the tunnel. It truly is one day at a time.

Incorporating Exercise for Health and Recovery

Although I diligently exercised prior to my stroke, I do not have the same desire to exercise now. I do understand its importance, so I strive to do some kind of exercise daily. In the hospital and on outpatient care, I had the encouragement and assistance of a therapist. Since the insurance company pays for only minimal assisted therapy, I struggle to motivate myself to exercise.

We don't all have the luxury of hiring a personal fitness trainer, but check into your local YMCA. Many of them offer a trainer to help you get started after your initial signup.

With insurance companies reducing or cutting off benefits, it leaves families wondering what to do. I knew this would eventually happen, so during my outpatient therapy sessions, I created a workbook of simple exercises that I could do on my own.

I had a friend take snapshots of me working with my therapist. The therapist wrote a sentence or two about each exercise. This helped immensely when I had to work alone at home. I have included some of those exercises in this section. I hope it will be of benefit to you.

As with any exercise program, don't start anything without first consulting your medical care provider.

An ongoing comment I receive from people around the country is, "My doctor has told me I won't get any better." The idea that a patient won't recover beyond six months after their stroke is, in my opinion, a myth. It is true that the sooner a patient can get into a rehabilitation program, the quicker their return of motor function. However, in my experience, I've seen stroke patients improve well beyond a year, post-stroke. I believe determination and persistence plays a major role.

I participated in a hands-on training program offered for the first time to physical therapy students at the University of Southern California (USC). Taking several survivors from my group, we committed to an hour and a half one day a week, for a twelve-week program. This was a wonderful opportunity, and it was free, giving us a chance to work on particular goals. We were videotaped at the beginning of the semester and again at the end to measure our progress.

The exercises on the following pages are part of a guideline that I use as a maintenance program. Covey Lazouras, a third year therapy student at the time with USC, was working with me every Tuesday, and graciously took part in these photos. Covey was fun and I learned a lot. Of course, he just happened to be young, tall, dark and handsome. Needless to say, I showed up every Tuesday!

Remember, what works for one person, may not work for another. Every stroke causes different injuries. Check with your doctor before trying any exercise.

A person's makeup, such as whether they are positive or assertive prior to their stroke, makes a definite difference in recovery. I know my body and its limitations. For me, I have found yoga combined with some bridging to be very beneficial. Again, I strongly stress checking with your doctor before starting an exercise program. Here are several beginning exercises to try.

Bridge Exercise ('Bed Pan') Exercise:

1. Lie on the floor, bed or mat with both knees bent up with your feet flat on the floor.
2. Your feet should be in a neutral position pointing forward.
3. As you lift up your buttocks, tighten your stomach and buttock muscles. Concentrate on keeping both hips evenly off the ground.
4. Hold for a count of ten and slowly bring your hips down. Remember that your upper back does not rise off the floor.
5. Try ten sets; then rest and repeat.

Hip-control Exercise (try a set of 10):
1. Lie on your back with both legs bent up, your feet in a neutral position.
2. Controlling the knee – slowly let the knee out.
3. Gradually return the knee to a neutral position.

Shoulder Range Motion (Superman position):
    For this exercise, you can use a broom handle or a wooden dowel from your local hardware store. This exercise can be done lying on your bed with your head hanging over the edge.
1. Lie on your stomach with your feet shoulder-width apart.
2. Make sure your neck is in a neutral position, looking down.
3. Raise the bar up to your shoulders, hold, then gradually back down. Your hands should be shoulder width apart.
4. Repeat 10 times.

Another exercise with the bar is to raise it to your chin with both elbows bent. You may have to bring your hands in closer. Control the bar as you slowly bring it down. This stabilizes your scapula.

Balancing:

Leaning over the ball, put your hands in position with your fingers spread evenly on the affected side. (This can be done without the ball.) Keep your elbows straight and your head in a neutral position. This exercise challenges all the muscles of the torso. It's a less threatening weight-bearing exercise on the joints. It enhances the muscles to work together through the hip and shoulder.

Weight-Bearing:
1. Leaning your torso over the ball, lift the strong arm.
2. Place all your weight on the affected arm. This is a good weight-bearing exercise.

Purchasing an exercise ball is a good investment. Your therapist can get it for you. The vinyl balls come in three different colors: green, orange and blue. Check with your therapist if this or any exercise is right for you.

The use of stretchable latex rubber bands for strength resistance is also extremely effective so check with your therapist for the appropriate resistance. The patient needs to be able to move through the range of motion 8 to 10 times.

For advanced exercises with the ball, make sure you have supervision.

At the Gym

Participating in some form of exercise on a daily basis improves us mentally and emotionally. I find my depression is less, and for me, being able to work out a little in a gym again makes me feel normal. This was a big part of my life prior to my stroke.

At my local gym, I try to do some muscle strengthening exercises for my lower extremities. I use the stair-master for weight bearing on my weak leg without the brace. I try to bear weight on my left hand while holding on; however, sometimes it helps to strap my hand on with an ace bandage. When I first started with this exercise, I could climb for only five minutes. I slowly built up to 30 minutes.

With the help of an assistant, I can ride a stationary bike for 30 minutes with my foot ace-bandaged to the pedal. The leg press machine is also very good but it is important that someone stabilize my knee and ankle while the brace is off. Recently, I have been able to do the leg press by myself on a lighter weight with more repetitions. I stabilize my knee so it doesn't wobble by placing a small ball between the knees and concentrating on putting weight through the leg.

As I stated earlier, always check with your doctor first, then do what works for you. I no longer feel that I have to build up a sweat to get a good work out. Since my stroke, I tire easily and, therefore, have to be careful not to overwork. Some days, I have more energy than others. Remember to be patient with yourself and take it easy.

Insurance Concerns

The recovery process begins almost immediately – while the patient is in ICU. It starts with simple range of motion exercises. Once the patient enters a rehabilitation program, the long road of recovery lies ahead. What has changed since I was in the hospital is the insurance company policies. Years ago a patient would have stayed in the hospital nine months recovering. Today, a patient is lucky to get six weeks.

Each insurance policy has certain criteria for rehabilitation. The government sets the criteria and a patient has to be able to perform a minimum of three hours of therapy in order to participate. The case manager needs to show that there is a team needed in order to make that recovery happen. The insurance companies are now making a decision whether or not a patient can enter a particular rehabilitation program.

When you are dealing with an insurance company, it is best to find out if they have a case manager assigned to the case. If a patient does not meet the criteria, the insurance company may put them into a skilled nursing program. Rehabilitation can be provided on several levels, starting out in the acute phase in the hospital where a therapist comes to the room. The patient is then transferred to a rehab program where he or she could receive, at the skilled nursing level, approximately one hour of therapy a day.

Acute rehabilitation is three hours of therapy a day, followed by a home health care program of several times a week. From there a patient goes into an outpatient program that is usually three times a week. A lot has changed with insurance companies and the level of authority for medical treatment that case managers once had.

Although people are suspicious of the insurance case managers, they can often be your best friends because they are the go-betweens for the adjuster and the medical team. It is a good idea to ask if there is a case manager involved because very often they will advocate for the patient even though they are on the insurance company's payroll.

It is insurance companies that make deals with hospitals. They pick the center of excellence bound by a contract. You have to accept those centers that have contracted with your insurance company; however, if you are not happy with the facility you do have the choice to change. I made some progress on a daily basis. My age affected the decision. My will to improve and get the best treatment possible for the best outcome also played a part.

Isa Anderson, past director of case management at Freeman Hospital, offers this advice: "The patient needs an advocate who is willing to stand up for them. It's an overwhelming process, however, there are things that can be done for the patient. The family member can sit down with a financial counselor at the hospital and review the patient's insurance policy. If they have difficulty in understanding the policy they can also review it with the insurance company membership advisor."

Ask if there is an insurance case manager assigned to the patient. Find out who it is and ask questions. The advocate needs to be as educated as possible on the patient's policy. Speak with the patient's human resource department and inquire about the benefits the patient had with that employer.

As always, "the squeaky wheel gets the grease." Don't be afraid to speak up. Familiarize yourself with your coverage and read the fine print. Know your doctor and develop a good relationship so you can be prepared.

My husband reminds families of survivors to ask questions, then ask more questions, and make demands when necessary. He recommends you do as he did: Always ask the doctors, point blank, "What would you do if this was your loved one?"

Try to find someone to be your personal advocate. Never try to do it alone. Never give up.

Rehabilitation and Recovery

It is helpful for family members to be assertive in asking questions, especially if they are not seeing results in the patient's recovery. Rehabilitation hospitals encourage the family's involvement because they may notice things that a doctor may not. A stroke survivor may not have any obvious physical disability but they may be having difficulty expressing themselves.

One man in my stroke group had trouble speaking and constantly had uncontrolled bursts of swearing. Another survivor could move fine, but had no feeling on the affected side. Some lose their ability to read, write or speak. What we have in common is the fact we have experienced a stroke. Knowing people who have gone down the same road and are there to support us can alleviate a stroke survivor's fears.

Frequently, in e-mails I receive from all over the world, I'm asked what the survivor may be feeling. It varies from individual to individual, depending upon what part of the brain has been affected. Ask questions of the patient's doctor and find out what kinds of problems you can expect from their stroke. If you don't understand, ask the doctor to explain it in layman terms. Statistics show that most recovery takes place in the first six months, yet my recovery continues on a daily basis and I am not alone in that respect. A patient has to be willing to put forth the effort and literally never give up.

The key to successful therapy is the patient must want to do the therapy. Often I receive letters from a caregiver asking why they cannot motivate the survivor to do the therapy. The motivation has to come from the survivors. Nagging them to do their therapy may only aggravate the problem.

Typically, when the stroke occurs on the left side of the brain, the right side of the body is affected. If the stroke is on the right side of the brain, the left side of the body is affected. Both have language and behavior problems. Problems with the left-brain stroke are usually aphasia and difficulty in understanding. The survivor has problems forming words, reading and writing.

Stroke sometimes creates strange phenomena. If, for example, the survivor loses their ability to speak English, they may be able to speak another language fluently if the other was their first language.

If the stroke affects the right side of the brain, the survivor will experience similar problems. In addition, there is often left side neglect and problems with simple tasks like dressing. Speech, reading and writing may also be affected. The patient will often have to be reminded when eating to chew or swallow their food. It's normal to see patients pocket their food in their mouths. Other problems include: short attention span, outbursts of anger, inappropriate laughter or crying and loss of musical abilities.

The best advice I could give to a family is to encourage the patient to do therapy. On occasion, I receive mail about a patient who is three years post-stroke and is now in a nursing home. The family is reaching out for help to see if they can get therapy for their loved one. These are often survivors who are in their twenties and were angry after their stroke that they refused to do therapy.

I can never emphasize enough that a patient has to be willing to do the therapy, do it early, and follow directions from the therapist. Often, it helps if the therapist talks with the family to offer suggestions as to what they can do to encourage the patient.

Sometimes it helps to have the doctor or social worker talk to the patient. Katrina, my occupational therapist suggested, "When patients are able to, have them sign a written contract that they will participate in therapy. This can help, allowing the patient some control in the decision-making. It is totally normal to be angry, but the patient shouldn't let their emotions interfere with their therapy," she says.

I know it's difficult. I constantly had to put my feelings aside in order to concentrate on my therapy.

Stroke and Emotions

During ICU and rehab, I constantly cried, which is a normal reaction from the brain damage occurring because of the stroke. In rehab I would frequently have bouts of crying which suddenly changed to bouts of uncontrollable laughter. My therapists knew to have me sit and finish out my cycle of laughter before continuing with therapy.

The inappropriate crying and laughing has diminished somewhat but only because I can control it. If I'm nervous I'll typically start laughing.

At times the family does not know how to deal with the patient's reactions and mood swings. In my own case, I wanted family and friends to just let me cry. I felt alone and there was nothing they could do to take my pain away. When patients can communicate after they stop crying, ask how you can help, and wait patiently for a response.

It is said that over time emotional lability will decrease with the recovery from stroke. I have not found this in my case. Most people who know me understand what's happening when I suddenly start laughing and can't stop. Sometimes I laugh so hard I have tears rolling down my face and people wonder what is so funny. I find the easiest way for me to cope is to let people know what's happening as soon as I can.

Dr. Saver suggests some medications that may help with emotional lability: (1) selective serotonin reuptake inhibitors, and (2) tricyclic antidepressants. He states that Baclofen has less supportive evidence and is more of a third line agent.

Before my stroke, I prided myself on being able to control my emotions. Now, the minute I think of something sad, I get tears in my eyes. If I'm not careful the tears turn to anguished sobs and no one knows why I am crying. What usually works for me is to think of something that makes me happy. Emotional lability is a common result of stroke.

Post-stroke depression is also a common side effect, and I speak with a lot of survivors who are trying to cope with it. During those first few months after the stroke, it's normal to feel like you are on a roller coaster with your emotions.

Both of my social workers assisted in helping me cope with these feelings and provided encouragement during my recovery. As with the loss of anything, you go through a grieving process. First there is the shock of having the stroke. Then you move through the different stages of denial, anger, guilt, depression and finally acceptance. The purpose of grieving is to allow someone to come to terms with his or her loss.

It's been several years since my stroke, and I still deal with bouts of depression. Depression pours in like a tidal wave at times, magnifying small concerns into major issues, like yearning to wear those cute shoes from the past. I often have to talk myself through the process. I'm disabled. I wear a brace; and no, those shoes aren't for me.

What I have learned about my depression is that it will pass. I acknowledge the feeling and wait until it leaves me. Although it may not be for everyone, I have found that a mild anti-depressant has helped balance me out. There have been occasions when I have tried to wean myself off the anti-depressant only to find that I start to sink into depression. I hope I don't have to be on this medication for a lifetime, but each person is different, and only you and your doctor can decide what is best for you.

Yes, I do believe in a positive attitude, but I have learned my limitations and try not to let myself get to the point of being so tired that I become angry. If I overwork myself one day, I know I'm going to pay the price the following day. Then I could become angry at something as simple as a person in the grocery store not pushing their cart through the check-out line.

Over the last few years I have accepted my disability, yet questions run through my mind. Will I have to deal with this disability the rest of my life? Is my left arm ever going to function normally? How am I going to feel in ten years? Even though these questions do haunt me, what I do know is what I have today and this moment. When I have those days I just feel blue and nothing seems to help, I focus on what I have, what I can do.

Stroke and Marriage

Strokes attack marriages too. I went through another bout of depression going through my divorce. I think anyone who faces divorce knows that it is a difficult and depressing process. Ninety percent of couples get divorced following a stroke.

A particular stroke survivor in my group had been a successful businessman. His wife divorced him because she felt he was no longer the man she married. They had been married for 17 years. It devastated him. I have heard many sad stories like this.

Like any other trial, stroke can also strengthen relationships. Both the stroke and divorce have made me a stronger person today. I had married couples in my stroke group where the disability had strengthened their relationship because there was a strong bond between them at the outset.

Stroke Support Groups

What seems to help me most with my depression is to focus on someone else and stay busy. When we focus on other people we don't have time to dwell on our own problems. That was one of my main reasons for starting a support group. I encouraged the people to reach out and help others. After a stroke, we often have feelings of worthlessness and hopelessness. By doing something simple to help someone else, we relieve ourselves of those feelings. My involvement with support groups, my board work, professional speaking and writing this book have all helped my recovery immensely. It has given greater purpose and meaning to my life than I had before the stroke.

The support group was successful because of those who gave freely and reached out to help others who were on their journey. In my own group I have seen people come in like wounded birds and regain their life. Having the support of others who can relate to their situation helps stroke survivors immensely.

While the patient is in outpatient therapy, ask the social worker to recommend a stroke support group. Ask if there is one that meets at the hospital. Once the patient is out of the hospital, finding support with others of similar circumstances will help. A younger survivor is dealing with different issues than an older survivor, especially if there are children involved. You may have to call around for a support group that meets those needs.

Sometimes the survivor is not ready to be in a group, so I encourage the family to come along and listen. It reassures survivors by going with them for the first few times before going to their groups alone.

Having support from others does not necessarily eliminate anger and frustration, but it does provide relief to know that we are not alone. Each of us gives one another the encouragement to carry on.

I love what Winston Churchill once said: "We make a living by what we get, but we make a life by what we give."

Out in the World

Today I'm able to enjoy many things again by taking advantage of the handicap provisions that come with my limitations. One is shopping. Going to a mall can be exhausting. I park as close to the store as possible in a handicapped parking space (if I can find one!). Most malls and large stores have an information desk where you can ask for a wheelchair. There have been times when I thought I could walk around in a mall, but found myself too tired to get back to my car. By simply asking for assistance, a wheelchair can be provided and security is only too happy to help.

Attitude plays a big part in recovery. It is true that 90 percent of what matters in recovery is attitude and that critical last 10 percent is just showing up.

Initially my goal was to walk out of the hospital. I wanted to achieve at least that level of independence, but it was not to be. It took another couple of months of hard work in outpatient therapy to get to that level of recovery.

What is a Stroke?

A stroke occurs when the blood flow to the brain is interrupted by a blocked or burst blood vessel. Depending on where the damage has occurred in the brain, rehabilitation will be different for each person.

Many people are confused by the myth that stroke only happens to older people. I can't tell you how many times people have said to me, "You're too young to have had a stroke." The majority of strokes happen to people 65 and older; however, it is not unusual for younger people to experience a stroke. Over 700,000 Americans suffer strokes each year (making stroke the third leading cause of death in the United States), 168,000 of them are under the age of 65. Stroke is the number one cause of disability. In this country someone experiences a stroke every 53 seconds. With the ongoing research and technology available today, many survivors are able to recover sufficiently to lead fulfilling lives.

Suffering a stroke is an emergency and time is precious. Below are listed stroke warning signs. If you are experiencing any of the following symptoms, call 911.

- Sudden weakness or numbness of the face or arm and leg on one side of the body.
- Sudden dimness or a loss of vision – in one or both eyes.
- Loss of speech or just trouble talking or understanding.
- Sudden and severe headaches with no apparent cause.
- Unexplained dizziness, unsteadiness or sudden falls, particularly if accompanied by any of the previous symptoms.

Many people experience a TIA (transient ischemic attack). This has some of the same symptoms as stroke but lasts anywhere from five minutes to 24 hours. A TIA should not be ignored, as this may be a warning of an impending stroke. According to the American Heart Association, a person who has a TIA is 9.5 times more likely to have a stroke.

Knowing the warning signs can help you reduce the damage a stroke can cause. A drug, TPA (Tissue Plasminogen Activator) can be administered to dissolve a clot in the brain reducing cell damage if given within the first three hours of the onset of a stroke. Although it is federally approved, it can only be used for ischemic strokes. Approximately 80 percent of strokes are ischemic, where there is a blockage in the blood vessels to the brain. The other kind of stroke is hemorrhagic, caused by a burst or leaking blood vessel in the brain or brainstem.

What is Aphasia?

Some survivors suffer aphasia, meaning they have difficulty in speaking and understanding. Often, they understand more than they can say. Some cannot write. "How can I help?" is a question the caregiver frequently asks when a patient seems to be having trouble communicating.

It is important to let the person with aphasia try to get the words out themselves. Try not to interrupt them. They can carry a small card explaining that they have trouble speaking. That way people will understand their situation and be more patient with them. Typically, people with aphasia will do better with short simple sentences. (The National Aphasia Association's telephone number is listed in the resource section. Contact them for more specific information.)

How to Prevent Stroke

What you don't know can not only hurt you, it can kill you. There are some measures you can take right now to lessen your chance of a stroke. We have all heard the Surgeon General's warnings about smoking. By choosing to stop, you greatly reduce your risk of cardiovascular disease. What about oral contraceptives? Women need to be assertive and ask questions at the doctor's office. They should make sure the doctor discusses the risk factor. They need to find out if they are a likely candidate for strokes and what steps they can take to lower their risk of cardiovascular disease.

Statistics show that more women die from cardiovascular disease each year than from breast cancer. Many women who smoke and take oral contraceptives increase their risk of a stroke 22 times more than average. Please don't smoke and take birth control pills. If you decide to smoke, oral contraceptives should be avoided. There is an increased risk of birth control pills or patch causing stroke if you have migraine headaches. Discuss with your doctor the risks and benefits of oral contraceptives and alternate methods of birth control.

Prior to my own stroke, I didn't ask questions. I assumed I was in good hands with my doctor. Today, I believe we must play an active role in our own health care. There are changes we can make in our lives to help prevent a stroke. We can lose weight, stop smoking, exercise on a regular basis and cut back on alcohol and sodium. No one knows our bodies better than us.

Turn Tragedy into Triumph

I have gone through the same grieving process that anyone who has been through a tragedy goes through. The lessons I have learned have been invaluable and made me a stronger, more empathetic person.

Thousands of survivors share a common bond of moving from helplessness to triumph. Although the ever-present question, "Why me?" may never be answered; one thing I feel strongly about, is that God is using my experience as a reminder to us all that life is precious. It is comforting to know that God is only a prayer away.

Congressional Speech

Congressional Speech

Delivered by Kate Adamson-Klugman
Before the Congress of the United States / April 23, 1997

Mr. Chairman, honorable members of the Committee, it is a privilege to speak to you today. My name is Kate, I am a spokesperson for the American Heart Association, and most importantly, I am a mother and a wife.

I know many people feel skeptical about Congress. Many people believe that government can do no good and that everything in Washington is all about the almighty dollar. I am here to say that they are wrong. You, as a body, have done great things for those unfortunate people who, through no fault of their own, are sick and in real need of real help. The Americans with Disabilities Act, and the help you have given to research, to prevent, cure and lessen the effects of stroke and heart disease, are some of the finest things to ever come out of any government.

I know you face hard challenges in today's world. What you spend here, you cannot spend there. You are faced with very, very difficult choices. But, the true measure of a society is how it treats the least of its members, how it cares for the sick and the needy.

I am only 34 years old, and before my devastating stroke in June of 1995, I was a mother, a wife, an athlete and person vitally interested in my community. Now, after suffering a double brainstem pons stroke, which left me totally paralyzed, unable to even blink, and after months and months of treatment, I am still a mother, a wife, and someone vitally interested in a broader community. Only now, I am all these things but without the use of the left side of my body.

Without the funding you have already given to fight stroke and heart disease, I would be none of these things. After my stroke, I suffered from Locked-in Syndrome. I spent fifty days in the ICU. During those 50 days, I was conscious, I could feel everything, I could feel pain, but I could not move any part of my body. I was totally trapped in my body. Fed by a tube surgically placed in my stomach, breathing only by using a tube surgically placed in my throat, I could not speak, could not eat, could not drink, and could not move from the rigid death-like position my body had assumed.

There was little hope for me to even live through the night, and frankly, my doctor hoped I would not live, since my future seemed so bleak. I am a very lucky woman. I lived, and more than that, I overcame Locked-in Syndrome.

My miracle did not come about without much prayer and great skill on the part of my doctors. The knowledge and skill my doctors possessed is something that this government, acting at its best, helped make possible. Without years of research and many dollars provided by men and women like you, I would not be here to talk to you today.

Of course, the story does not end with my leaving the ICU; it only begins there. I have been through countless hours of therapy. Physical therapy has been developed to its present stage with the help of funds provided in part by this government.

I have seen my own life come to a point where I could do nothing for myself. I found myself at 33 wearing a diaper and unable to control my own bodily functions. I saw myself unable to talk for months. All the communication I had with the outside world was limited to blinking my eyes either yes or no. I will not mention the physical pain, for it was transitory.

Were you to see my daughters' tears, 18-month-old Rachel and 3-year-old Stephanie, it would be enough to convince you to make research funding one of your top priorities. If you could see what this has done to my husband and other friends you would realize that stroke and heart disease is not just a problem that strikes one person, it strikes families and whole communities.

Every minute in the United States someone suffers a stroke. Annually, stroke effects more people than cigarette smoking kills. Each year over 500,000 people have a stroke. Nearly a third will die within a few months. Almost all of the survivors will be disabled for the rest of their lives.

The treatment of stroke will cost this nation over twenty-five billion dollars in medical costs and approximately two hundred billion more in lost productivity. If we hope to save Medicare, which is one of this Congress' top priorities, we must learn to spend medical dollars wisely. With research, we can prevent and cure stroke thus saving billions of dollars and, in the bargain, saving innocent people from a living death.

There is no greater good that you, as a Congress, could possibly do than to help the dedicated men and women who fight daily to prevent and to cure stroke and heart disease. I pray you will generously help us.

I will close by asking you to be just a little selfish, for if I can stand here today, when yesterday I was the picture of health, so can you stand here tomorrow also the victim of stroke. I pray it will not happen to you, but the truth is within the next ten years it will happen to some of you, and it may happen to all of you. So please, help, for in helping any of us, you will help all of us.

Kate Adamson-Klugman

Kate participating in 5K walk.

How to Survive a Medical Crisis

by Steven Klugman

The best way to survive a medical crisis is to not have one. "A stitch in time saves nine." "An ounce of prevention is worth a pound of cure." These sayings are trite because they have been spoken a lot, because they are true. Staying healthy is the best prevention. Eat healthy, exercise, and get regular medical check-ups. Kate is alive today in no small part because she was fit.

I was Kate's caregiver and advocate throughout her ordeal. There are a number of things I learned that might help you survive the maze of regulations, doctors, therapists and insurance providers.

This may be a difficult time for you, but you must step up for the sake of your loved one. Be empathetic and loving, yes, but also be strong and rational. You cannot help in this crisis if you are hysterical.

The first thing you must do is gather information. When Kate had her stroke, I had lots of questions, but no answers. I didn't know what a stroke was. I had to gather information in a hurry, but I managed because I had once given some serious thought to the idea that I might someday face a medical crisis of my own. I assumed that something might happen to me, not Kate, because I was older and out of condition, while she was in excellent shape. I had pre-established relationships with doctors I trusted. I knew a good cardiologist, a good neurologist and more than one good lawyer.

I was prepared to get as many opinions as I might need. Everyone believes that doctors know everything, everyone that is but doctors. Competent doctors are not offended if you want a second opinion, so don't hesitate to ask for one. Your doctor does not know everything and will often recommend other doctors from whom you can get a second opinion. Regardless of your financial situation, you have every right to ask questions. Getting things right from the beginning is much better than trying to fix things after they have gone wrong.

The best way to get thoughtful information from a doctor is to ask, "What would you do if this was your wife or child?" "What kind of specialist would you consult?" "Who is the best doctor for this situation?" Question them and if they don't know something, find out who does. You may need to be persistent. If this is difficult for you, find someone to help you; a relative or a friend or, if you can afford one, an attorney.

You must know what you want to accomplish in order to accomplish anything. Is your situation serious but not hopeless? Is surgery or specialized treatment needed but unavailable due to lack of funds? There are many medical miracles out there, but the real miracle is paying for them. Get clear with the doctor about possible treatments and how much they cost. Remember, doctors want to help, but medicine is a business and businesses exist to make a profit, or they cease to exist, and then they can't help anyone. The money issue must be faced squarely and quickly.

If you don't know where to find information, try the internet. If you're not computer savvy, find a friend who is, or check out the resources listed in this book. You are welcome to contact us at kate@kateadamson.com and we will offer you direction.

If you understand what your options are, decide what the best possible outcome is. For me, that was having Kate make a total and complete recovery. I knew that at some point I might have to change my goals, but at this early stage I decided I would insist on nothing less than full recovery.

This was not easy because no one agreed with me. The doctors felt I was unrealistic. That was okay. I meant to be unrealistic – and (at least initially) so should you. If you don't try for the best you have little chance of getting it.

As you know, from reading Kate's book, the doctors did not believe that treatment would produce results anywhere near worth the cost of the treatment. They had a point. Kate ultimately cost me and the insurance company in the neighborhood of 2 to 2.5 million dollars. Who would think that Kate was worth 2.5 million dollars? The insurance company didn't. I did. I still do. I was unrealistic but had I not been, I would be a widower.

I knew that I could lower my expectation in the future if it was ever necessary. Initially it was best to shoot high. You may have to change your plan later, but at least start with expectations for the best possible outcome.

Get an honest assessment from the doctors as to what the odds are with your medical situation. The odds are just that, odds. The doctors said that Kate's chances were a million to one. I focused on the one – not the million.

Make sure your doctors are on your side. It's best if they want to help you because they agree with your hope in the outcome. If they don't share your hope, try to get them to cooperate because it is the right thing to do. If you are faced with having one-in-a-million odds, this may be difficult. That's okay, just let them know you understand that you face long odds. Ask them to tell you the truth and to keep you informed but to leave room in their minds for a miracle. Let them know you, too, are willing to change your mind as things develop, but ask them to respect your wishes for now.

I did have a reputation for being a bit of a nuisance, but this was a matter of life and death, and I was not about to lose the fight because I was afraid of offending someone. If you need to, don't hesitate to go the head nurse or above. Remember, you are the customer. If it feels wrong – change it.

The most important people to have on your side are the nurses. They are generally easier to enlist than other medical professionals. It may be that there is less ego to deal with, I don't know. I found that the nurses are almost always the ones most willing to help.

You are going to need the nurses' help on a continual basis. They will be the first one to see progress and you need them to record and chart each progress. Be a part of the team and let them know that you willing to help. If the staff sees that you come from love, not ego, you will be given greater latitude. Without the support of a great nursing staff, I could not have been effective. I will always be grateful for the help the nurses gave me in convincing the doctors to treat Kate as well as they ultimately did.

Sometimes, though, you have to be feared instead of loved. When you meet resistance, carry a clip board with you like I did and write things down. Be obvious. Let people know that you are watching and documenting everything. Sometimes, it is the fear of being sued that motivates people.

Get to know the day and night nurses, the head nurse, the attending physicians, case manager, social worker, insurance adjuster and others. Keep their names and phone numbers readily available.

Call your list occasionally reminding them about the patient and inform them of any progress or problems. Don't assume that everyone knows what is going on. Encourage all the members of the team to talk to each other. Keep everyone aware of the entire picture.

Each night before you go to bed review what happened that day. What worked and what did not work? What was the miracle of the day? What good things did you see that you can use to encourage yourself? You must also acknowledge mistakes or problems. Before I went to sleep I would list the problems in my mind and literally sleep on possible solutions. When Kate was growing her antibiotic resistant infection, I would often awaken with several courses of action.

I strongly recommend being there when the doctor makes the daily rounds. This may be the only time each day that the doctor is going to see the patient and it is your best chance to get information. How are the patient's vital signs? What progress has been made since yesterday? What is the most significant problem the patient faces today? Do we need new treatments or medications? What do you recommend? Do we need second opinions? Are you having any problems with the insurance company? What can I do to help?

It's your job to help your loved one be as positive and proactive as possible. You must establish trust. Be honest. Don't sugar coat bad news, but be sure and emphasize good news. Sometimes, things are not going to work out well and you have to deal with it. It is up to you to decide if you will be the bearer of bad tidings or if you will rely on the doctor to do that.

Everyone does not have private insurance but, in almost all cases, someone else is paying for the medical treatment. Some principals apply to private and public insurance. Usually someone will have to plead your case in order to get the necessary treatment. It might be your case manager, your doctors, an attorney or you.

You have to find out what the insurance will and will not do (when I say insurance company, I include government plans like Medicare and MediCal). Whatever the proposal, there is going to be someone who says "yes" or "no" to the requested care. It depends on their interest in the matter and that interest is often financial.

The less the insurance company pays the more money they save. The more care approved by the insurance company the more the hospital stands to make. The bottom line is that it is vitally important to get the insurance company to provide an authorization to provide care. Every company has a set of rules that, in most cases, they will follow. Still there is always some leeway.

Your first job is to find out what the standards and procedures are that apply to you. This is where a lawyer may come in, or a good friend. The one person you must establish a good relationship with is the case manager. Kate and I have been asked on many occasions to help out with this type of issue and we have been able to achieve some satisfying results.

Make sure your loved one knows you are there for them through thick and thin. Try to find out what the patient needs then set up a support system that will help. The patient may not want a lot of visitors – or any at all. Sometimes encouraging cards and letters is all that is needed or wanted. Do not exhaust the patient or nurses with unnecessary contact, especially during critical stages of recovery.

Most importantly remember to take care of yourself or you will not be able to take care of anyone else. Caring for the patient is best accomplished by caring for the caregiver.

Give people an idea of what you need and don't be afraid to ask for help. Spend as much support time as you can but don't feel guilty about having to be somewhere else. If you have to work, you have to work. If your kids need you then be there for them. Do the best you can.

Also realize you did not cause the illness and you cannot fix it. If you have spiritual beliefs, this is a good time to rely on God's blessings. Ultimately it is in God's hands, so do your best each day and leave the day behind when you go to sleep.

Resources

AHA (American Heart Association)
www.americanheart.org

AMERICAN PHYSICAL THERAPY ASSOCIATION
800-999-2782
www.apta.org

AMERICAN SPEECH, LANGUAGE AND HEARING ASSOC.
800-638-8255
www.asha.org

AMERICAN STROKE ASSOCIATION
888-4-Stroke (478-7653)
www.StrokeAssociation.org
Stroke Connection Magazine
Free for survivors and caregivers
800-553-6321
Email: strokeconnection@heart.org

AMERICAN STROKE FOUNDATION
866-549-1776
www.americanstroke.org

AMERICANS WITH DISABILITIES ACT
800-514-0301
www.ADA.gov

BRAIN INJURY ASSOCIATION
703-761-0750
800-444-6443 (Information line)
www.biausa.org

KATE'S JOURNEY CONSULTING
Professional Speaking, Patient Advocacy and Assistance
800-641-KATE (5283)

NATIONAL APHASIA ASSOCIATION
800-9224622
www.aphasia.org

NATIONAL REHABILITATION INFORMATION CENTER
800-346-2742
www.naric.com

NATIONAL STROKE ASSOCIATION
800-787-6537
www.stroke.org
Stroke Smart Magazine
Free for survivors and caregivers

SAFE: STROKE AWARENESS FOR EVERYONE
www.StrokeSAFE.org

STROKE ASSOCIATION OF SOUTHERN CALIFORNIA
310-575-1699
www.strokesocal.org

THE STROKE NETWORK, INC.
www.StrokeNetwork.org

TERRI SCHINDLER SCHIAVO FOUNDATION
727-490-7603
www.terrisfight.org

WELL SPOUSE ASSOCIATION
800-838-0879
www.wellspouse.org

Driving

AARP (American Association of Retired People)
www.aarp.org/families/driver_safety

DRIVER'S ED ORGANIZATION
Will assist individuals in finding programs in their area
Can serve as a resource for equipment
Toll Free 877-529-1830
www.driver-ed.org

DRIVING SCHOOL ASSOCIATION OF CALIFORNIA
Frank Boutelle
951-515-5125
www.dsac.com

About the Author

The lessons Kate learned through her miraculous recovery from total paralysis provide a practical as well as inspirational example for any individual or company who feels paralyzed in reaching their goals and aspirations.

Corporations, hospitals, nurses, medical groups, and government agencies bring Kate to their conventions to inspire their audiences to recognize and overcome paralysis that keeps them from moving to their next level. Her powerful message focuses on what they can do, not what they can't.

She is an amazing, unique keynote speaker, traveling from coast to coast with a message of inspiration and hope. Her award winning book has touched countless lives, encouraging those who experience overwhelming challenges and feel paralyzed.

Since her devastating stroke, she has accomplished more than anyone could imagine. She is an outspoken advocate for every individual's right to live and be recognized as a contributing human being despite disabilities.

A popular resource for the media, Kate has appeared on national radio and television, including CBS Sunday Morning

News, Fox News, The O'Reilly Factor, The Abrams Report, MSNBC, ABC, 700 Club, Coral Ministries and the Trinity Broadcast Network. She has appeared on CNN, Paula Zahn Now, and Larry King Live.

Her story and book have been featured in national magazines including *Redbook, Vim & Vigor, Caregiver, Keeping Well, Prevention, Stroke Smart, Stroke Connection,* and *The Female Patient.*

Kate has served as a national spokesperson for the American Stroke Association and a board member of the South Bay American Heart Association in Los Angeles. She serves on the board for the Stroke Association of Southern California and was appointed to the University of Southern California, Division of Biokinesiology and Physical Therapy Board of Counselors. Kate is a tireless advocate for patient's rights and women's health. Focusing on abilities instead of disabilities, she is a powerful advocate for 'Ability Awareness' and 'Appreciation before Accommodation.' She has testified before the United States Congress in support of funding for stroke and heart research.

Born in New Zealand, she now lives in Los Angeles, with her husband and two daughters. She is available for speaking engagements at conferences and conventions. Contact her by visiting her website, kateadamson.com or email kate@kateadamson.com

What others are saying about all versions of this book:

Kate's Journey is inspiring and informative. I highly recommend it for health professionals. This book effectively counters the conventional wisdom that after a severe stroke a person's life is over. Kate demonstrates that determination and strength of will are the most important elements of a rehabilitation program.

– James Gordon, EdD, PT, FAPTA,
Associate Dean and Chair University of Southern California,
Division of Biokinesiology and Physical Therapy

I added Kate Adamson to my list of heroes. Her life of courage and tenacity is an inspiration.

– Susan Jeffers, PH.D
Feel the Fear and Do it Anyway

I hope people will read your book because it will help them very much.

– Art Buchwald

Kate's Journey allowed me to really understand the impact that we as healthcare professionals have on people who have incurred catastrophic events.

– Covey J. Lazouras, PT, DPT, NCS

If you ever wonder if miracles are real. Kate's story will renew your faith.

– Jay Jones / Television host and producer,
Trinity Broadcasting Network

A profoundly moving story. A message of hope and inspiration.

– Gregory J.P. Godek
1001 Ways to be Romantic

Kate's Journey won't make you think about how much better off you are than someone else [it] will help you be much better than you were.

– W Mitchell, CPAE
It's Not What Happens To You,
It's What You Do About It.

A mesmerizing inspirational story of courage and determination.
— Jane Harman, Congress of the United States

An inspiring read. A gift of hope.
— Debbie Allen,
Confessions of Shameless Self Promoters

Wonderful, inspiring, encouraging, and much needed in the world.
— Dottie Walters, CSP, International Speaker
Speak and Grow Rich

Compelling, gripping. Kate's faith in God and her testimony is a blessing to the body of Christ.
— Zac Nazarian, Senior Pastor,
Hope Chapel, Hermosa Beach, CA

An inspiration. An awesome testimony to hope and perseverance. We all must fight for the voiceless and be the Stevens in other people's lives.
— Chris Ice, Covenant Hospice Services

Share the Journey

You may order autographed copies of

Paralyzed but not Powerless

by calling
1-800-641-KATE (5283)
or ordering online
KateAdamson.com

Invite Kate to speak:

1-800-641-KATE (5283)

Your comments matter:

Please email your comments about the book to
Kate@KateAdamson.com